HOPE
Overcomes
FEAR!

HOPE
Overcomes
FEAR!

SANDRO MOTTA *and* SÔNIA MOTTA

MILL CITY PRESS

Mill City Press, Inc.
2301 Lucien Way #415
Maitland, FL 32751
407.339.4217
www.millcitypress.net

Unless otherwise indicated, Scripture quotations taken from the King James Version (KJV) – *public domain*.

Printed in the United States of America.

Paperback ISBN-13: 978-1-6628-1179-1
Ebook ISBN-13: 978-1-6628-1180-7

DEDICATION
and
ACKNOWLEDGMENTS

This book is dedicated to all readers, so that the glorious presence of Jesus Christ, our Savior, Lord and Friend, who is the Author and Finisher of our Faith and the Owner of life, be revealed with God's illuminating glory.

ACKNOWLEDGMENTS

To the Eternal God and Jesus Christ, to whom we declare our immense love, and the Holy Spirit who inspired us to write this book, perfecting our call to serve in His Good Work and in the Propagation of His Gospel, for Revival and Salvation!

To our daughter Vitória who motivated us to win before her birth.

To our dear mothers, Lídia and Enedina who pray so much for us, and in memory of our parents Jaciran and Ataide, for the heritage of their good teachings that will accompany us forever.

In memory of our extraordinary and unforgettable friend, Alceu.

To our sister Thais for her caring and motivating smile.

To our niece Jessica for being so helpful.

To our family, relatives and friends of the Faith.

To our faithful friend Márcio, who helped us so much to get here.

To our incredible brother, the great Guilherme, who is part of this journey and a friend in "battle".

For our righteous Brother Antônio, "Tonho", for always being honest with us.

To our accountant and friend Junior, his family and team, for all their dedication and support.

To our special friends Hercídio, Eliane, Matheus, Letícia and their families, with whom we live unforgettable moments.

To Sérgio and his family for their precious mindfulness.

To Robson for his loyal support.

To our Friend Lauma for her constant dedication.

To the helpful, always welcoming Osvaldo and his family.

To Ralph for his prayers and all goodwill towards our family, since we met.

To the loving and welcoming Lifebridge CHURCH family.

To the HARVEST English Institute and its competent team.

To our very special English teacher, super Eric.

To Adélia for her efficient and dedicated professionalism.

To our friends Daniel, his wife Michele, his children Gustavo, Felipe and Arthur, an invaluable family.

To the unforgettable Ricardo, Juliana, Super Levi, the incredible Gabi and her family.

To Jeff, Erica and the entire Xulon Press team, Mill City Press (Salem Media Group).

To all who kept us in their prayers and helped us in some way.

Sandro Motta & Sônia Motta

TABLE OF CONTENTS

TO ALL

Faith is a mystery and yet we understand that it is a great power given to us by God. It dwells within each one of us, to generate the power of thought, bringing into our dimension things into existence everything we need and truly believe, as if it already existed. Thus Hope is born in our Lives!

Believe and take possession of the words that JESUS CHRIST inspired the Apostle Paul to write, to leave us as an inheritance, in the New Testament Gospel of our Bible, where it is written:

> *"...knowing that tribulation worketh patience, and patience, experience; and experience, hope"*

> **Romans 5:3A - 4**

Chapter 1

DEFEATING ANXIETY

From ancient times to the present day, Kings, Princes, Governors, Great Leaders, Conquerors of the richest of all nations to the poorest commoners have all suffered, suffer, or will suffer from anxiety.

Our observation in this matter is that throughout the history of humanity, all lasting dominance exercised by the leaders who wrote it, by those who write it, and even by those who will write it, first experienced, or will experience it through personally studying, and understanding the full knowledge of the meaning utilizing the word that makes up our language.

* Whoever masters the WORD and believes and practices the meaning contained in it possesses a solid basis of communication, exercises strong influence, has free access to the source of strength to overcome and consequently the incredible power to win!

Let us analyze all the characteristics of our "silent adversary," anxiety, a noun with synonyms that give names to the main symptoms and damage that it causes us, with its scientific spectrum with the most complex aspect.

Let's zero in on our target!

We will proceed steadily to our target so that we may find the greatest force that is within each of us, unveiling all the weaknesses of anxiety, completely dominating it until we defeat it completely!

Anxiety is:

- Impatience - lack or absence of patience, agitation, nervousness, always present in the behavior of the person who cannot, does not know, or simply does not like to wait.

- Concern - preoccupied, exaggerated prevention, erratic anticipated opinion, a fixed idea that disturbs the spirit to the point of producing physical, mental, emotional suffering, and low self-esteem causing insecurity until it causes depression.

- Restlessness - disturbance, state of concern; restlessness that prevents rest, takes away peace, blocks and removes tranquility; the restless state of those suffering from agitation, nervousness.

- Agony - intense, strong, and profound suffering, equal to that pain felt in the last moment of life that precedes death (this being the biggest and most common symptom found in the behavior of those who unfortunately commit suicide).

• Affliction - persistent feeling of physical pain, mental, emotional, or moral suffering (causing low self-esteem), anxiety, agony, anguish

• Anguish - "a prison of the soul and sadness of the spirit," deep emotional pain, intense anxiety, restlessness; suffering, torment; psychological sensation characterized by suffocation, "tightness in the chest," extreme insecurity causing a distressed spirit.

• Panic - despair, terror, and fear which scares or frightens, with motives or even for no apparent reasons (such as panic syndrome ...).

Based on the seven words that depict what you just read of the main meanings of seven of the many evil words that are synonymous, define, and also answer what anxiety is and what it causes us. We will reflect, learn, and fix the perfect tactic, to eliminate it once and for all of our lives?

After all, what is anxiety for each of us?

How and when does it attack us?

To broaden our view of the topic, let's do a quick review with a "magnifying glass."

Considering that almost all the various questions and their answers on this topic are similar, it is worth highlighting a summary that we have edited especially so that we can better examine certain points and eliminate all the symptoms that an-xi-e-ty causes.

They are:

- "Great malaise in the "soul," emotional, physical and psychological pain, deep sadness; restlessness, acute distress, agony, despair."

- "Emotional, physical and psychological suffering; apathy, discouragement; restlessness, distress, agony, anguish, strong sadness; insecurity, panic, anxiety, nervousness."

- Psychological confusion, fragile or debilitated emotional state with a behavioral imbalance in the face of certain risk, and uncertain or dangerous future, in the face of difficult circumstances of life in which an individual feels very weak, totally impotent, helpless, unable to react proactively to defend himself better, being "blind" - without seeing a way out or solving one or more "problems," in addition to the other serious and important issues that require immediate action, motivated most of the time by strong decisions or choices that you will have to make.

- The term anxiety comes from the Greek "*Anshein*," which means suffocating or oppressing. The anguish has been related to its expression of something, in particular, an exclusive and very personal experience. Both the words suffocate or oppress, and anguish are always associated with somatization - the sensation of pain and physical symptoms arising from emotional, psychological disorders differentiated by their specific manifestations to each individual's body's reactions suffering from some type of an-xi-e-ty or even anxiety disorder.

- The word anxiety in Latin was influenced by the Greek and had the etymology - lat anxietas, which also means "anguish," "anxiety," from *anxius* = "disturbed," "uneasy," "from anguere" like "squeeze," "suffocate." That is why the meaning of the word anxiety in Latin is similar in concept to the Greek.

- Also, as the Greek-influenced the evolution of social communication, it is understandable that the meaning of this word has been translated in the same way in other languages. Which only makes it easier for us to identify its fragility, destroy its effects faster and eliminate all anxiety regardless of the different nations, languages, cultures, and people no matter where we originated from or belong.

*The **"source of anxiety is fear;"** as we just identified within its meaning and synonyms.

We can also say that fear is rooted in anxiety. Therefore, we can safely say and understand that "fear is born out of anxiety."

From this point forward, we can apply what we have learned about the behavior and even the weaknesses of the adversary of our dreams, plans, and successes. How about we fight it?

With the wisdom we've acquired through research, knowledge, and understanding, we now have a "weapon" that helps us master the words that define anxiety. We can overcome it!

With these "weapons," we can defend ourselves against it daily. We will unveil each powerful word that opposes it until it is totally defeated, and that day is today. We will start here and now, acting with the following virtues to overcome fear.

Such virtues are ours and have always been within us. The time has come to take possession of their strong meaning and immense power contained in the words that materialize these virtues:

- **Courage** - Courage is the strength and determination to overcome fear, break barriers and obstacles, adversities or challenges; a motivated, strong attitude, good spirits, firmness and integrity, fearlessness in the face of danger; bravery, strength of spirit, impetus, boldness, resolute decision that does not go back in the face of the risks foreseen in the most diverse and difficult circumstances of life.

- **Patience** - Patience and tolerance; perseverance; tranquility. Above all, patience is a virtue-based on our emotions' self-control, and that self-control begins in the mind, where our thoughts are born. It is also the quality of that which withstands strong pressure without losing its balance in adverse, unpleasant situations, in injuries, and other discomforts they suffer. That person has the ability to wait for what is taking without losing his calm, concentration, faith, and hope that he will receive or achieve his purpose.

- **Benevolence:** Benevolence is benignity, kindness, goodwill of spirit towards something or someone. Magnanimity mainly towards those under his guidance or command; complacency, compromise, altruism, ready willingness to help and help the needy, favorable to defend and support the innocent, abundant in compassion and mercy.

- **Calmness:** Certainly calm is peace of mind, patience, and temperance, long-suffering, placidity, peace; it's the calm that is found most quickly when we are resting, the eternal sleep of restlessness or agitation. The wealth of peace is a particular or peculiar character of those who are peaceful; quality and virtuosity of those seeking lasting peace—complacency, stillness, discipline, organization. Calm is also the principle of balance.

- **Balance:** Balance is having self-control. It is calm, uniformity, unity, convergence, and synergy, a condition of a system in which the acting forces compensate, mutually canceling every difference, generating a strong, stable body position, without oscillations or deviations, total harmony, and inner peace.

- **Meekness:** Meekness is consolidated calm as the main characters in the behavior of those who are calm. Full serenity, quality, or condition of those who are meek, mildness of genius, affection, temperance, balance, softness. Meekness is the virtue found at the root of love.

Peace - Peace is the expression of LOVE!!!

✓ In Latin *Pax*, it is generally defined as a state of strong calm and immense tranquility, especially in the relationship between people who are not in conflict.

✓ It is the absence of "problems" of disturbance or agitation. Also derived from the Latin *Pacem = Pacem Belli*, it can mean the absence of violence or war.

✓ An agreement, concord, harmony, unity and uniformity between Citizens and Nations...

☐ *After our "immersion" into the powerful meaning of these words of truth, it is wonderful to discover that we can overcome the fullness of the virtues that shine an intense light of wisdom in all of us.*

☐ *This is how we acquire magnificent strength that teaches us to cultivate and practice full knowledge. We can handle all that wisdom with the divine intelligence that makes us win. Allied to the immense supernatural power that we have conquered to overcome and defeat all anxiety, we dare to stand up against it in our lives.*

✓ *From now on, after this important victory, we will also discover:*

☐ *The Incredible!*

☐ *Fantastic!*

☐ *And the Extraordinary "SELF DOMAIN," which is one of the greatest powers we have, for "building the path" that will lead us to victory over all the fears we face, the difficult circumstances and even the worst adversities, those that cause tribulations opposing the good quality of our lives.*

Chapter 2

* GAINING SELF DOMAIN *

From sunrise to sunset, how many times are we challenged? From the moment we wake up and open our eyes until we close them and go to sleep?

We are confronted every day!

The different circumstances of life, obstacles, challenges, difficulties, tribulations that provoke us to react and impels us to overcome so that we are perfected and become better than before.

- When we overcome what happens inside and outside each of us, how can it positively influence everything and everyone around us?

- The truth is that it is wonderful when we win! It is an explosion of happiness and a magical moment! A great sense of power comes with the conquest, and immense self-confidence that takes hold of us for the new triumph achieved. It radiates and spreads to everything and everyone near us. In this extraordinary moment, we need to intensify the vigilance of our impulses, emotions, and attitudes, exercising Self-Control. This immense victory is a true blessing. It's focused and committed to not permitting the poison of vanities to contaminate us with pride and arrogance. It is so harmful to harmony and the maintenance of our success.

- Every experience is fantastic, when we act wisely!

- And when we lose: how do we react to the loss, and how do those around us react?

What happens is that when we lose, everything seems to end. It's because deep in our sub-conscious, we believe that we are not born to lose, right?

- Ah, but that's another story!

As we saw in the previous chapter, "DEFEATING anxiety," we will reconsider here and now aiding us to continuing our study of the 7 pillars:

- Courage!

- Patience!

- Benevolence!

- Calmness!

- Balance!

- Meekness!

- Peace!

Together, help us defeat anxiety and are the same that constitutes "SELF DOMAIN." Besides being the virtues of power for "building the path" of every victory, there are also hidden "keys" that will open after each journey. It's portals that keep the great secret behind our full and true triumph over fear.

Countless sources point us to the most similar and even the most different and varied definitions of its practical concept. However, we overcame all our old and fragile impulsivity when we were perfected in discernment, dominating our temperament. We start to act with all common sense, right after reflecting on the facts and experiences that helped shape our understanding of each emotion of this life. Giving us more capacity to perceive the difference between right and wrong, in addition to all lucidity, the strength and attitude to overcome our limits and triumph when great difficulties confront us, provoking and even "tempting" us.

There are many temptations to which we are subjected all the time. From the most varied and sophisticated forms to the simplest of temptation. The fact is, without exception, we are all tempted. It's at that moment of temptation, if we don't watch properly, keep our guard up, we will begin to get distracted with the seduction and the illusion of temptations, we will lose focus, and we may fall.

- How should we protect ourselves from something so unexpected?

- What apparently comes in such an "irresistible" way?

- Both in the field of imagination and with something much stronger, which is human vanities interference. It's the greatest trap hidden within us, and it is through them that humanity is defeated.

- From the beginning of creation, the history of humanity's trajectory is marked by temptations. It also proves to us how far and how great and dangerous the follies of human vanities are.

As surprising and incredible as it may seem, temptations can serve us to be perfected.

All of this and much more that happens around us has a purpose; we can actually discover something new at every moment:

- Things that strengthen us!

- Things that make us grow!

- Things that make us win!

- We can also learn what makes us lose.

- Things that weaken us.

- Things that bring us intense stress levels, where we will only overcome such an "attack" if we act quickly, with enough strength that keep us focused and the balanceds.

- **It is exactly there that the power of SELF DOMAIN comes into action in the life of each one of us. Which is our strong counterattack that rages, destroys, cancels, and defeats all our temptations.**

What is "SELF DOMAIN" in its practical concept?

In practice, "SELF DOMAIN" is the self-control we exercise over ourselves; it is the strength and power of knowing how to control our emotions or attitudes; it is discernment:

The ability to perceive the difference between right and wrong, rejecting, fighting and overcoming all evil, making the right choice, practicing GOOD, "in the name of what is just."

Always defending, preserving and protecting, what is good, what is perfect, and what is pleasing to the good quality of our lives and the lives of others.

Influencing and causing great benefit in the environment in which we live, building "bridges" that lead us to true PEACE!

After all, how can we own and practice **SELF DOMAIN**, day by day and invest it effectively in our lives?

- First, with all simplicity, we must maintain the discipline of <u>fighting and overcoming an-xi-e-ty, at all times, every day. Until our behavior of overcoming anxiety becomes so natural and spontaneous, "like the air we breathe." It's from that point on that it becomes an integral, inseparable, and spontaneous part of our body's defense system. * This is the principle of SELF DOMAIN.*</u>

In doing so, it is possible to develop and adopt a fascinating proactive attitude of power that cancels out the terrible and "lethal" impulsivity, allowing us to think before acting, keeping us firm and focused, ready and willing to listen and slow to speak.

* **Meditation** is an old tactic that can be ben-
eficial and effective in **exercising** to keep our
SELF DOMAIN alive.*

•   **What is Meditation?**

✓   After researching, interpreting, and practicing, we believe, there is a very simple
and at the same time particular, special,
personal, that the best meaning of the
word Meditation, looking through its
Latin root *meditare* - The notion to return
to a central point, right inside our BEING,
totally disconnecting from the dimension
of the outside world and "focusing on
ourselves," raising our mind to the state
of absolute concentration, peace, and
harmony, to connect "in spirit," with the
spark of GOD, which dwells within us.
This Divine spark is our true essence; the
vital force; the immortal portion, which
reflects the powerful presence of GOD in
our lives.

We understand that each of us can and should dedicate our time freely, in a very personal way and in a preferred place where we can best identify, in a sober and well-balanced way, to discover who we are, where we came from, and where we are going to return to. After we are perfected, our journey comes to an end when we leave behind the need to "have" **and are transported to the dimension of a new beginning, where we will become the incorruptible Image and Likeness of GOD, immortal and invulnerable. Like our original ancestors, Adam and Eve were created. Long before the temptation contaminated them to disobedience, which attacked and sabotaged the Garden of Eden that was with a total absence of need.**

This is the true heritage that has been restored by JESUS CHRIST, through his definitive sacrifice, by His matchless LOVE for all of us.

Now, coming back to the present to analyze today:

In a society with an increasingly larger, more digital and globalized population, where "everything is for yesterday." We must wake up and use our "SELF DOMAIN," which is within each of us, with much more intensity. If we want to prosper in all the functions and meanings of this word, we need to survive the turbulence, preserve, overcome challenges, and transform our lives.

There is a special ancient power born well before there was time itself, in the dimensions that we know or think we know. We will discuss this in a later chapter, and we believe you will be surprised! Together we will contemplate such power to consolidate this search, "crowning" our understanding with greater knowledge!

Let's solidify Meditation's meaning and practice. Meditation impels us, strengthens us, and improves us to dominate our temperament and keep our vision sharp, making us see much further and beyond what we can imagine.

SELF DOMAIN is the essential power to safely exercise the greatest gift of life, which is FREEDOM!

Chapter 3

* EXERCISING THE STRENGTH OF SELF-ESTEEM *

From now on, how about we take a deep deep breath, filling our lungs, bringing the STRENGTH OF SELF-ESTEEM to our lives? ...

You are invited to make this new, different, and impactful journey searching for this POWER so that together we find this EXTRAORDINARY STRENGTH, this DYNAMO!

It's a MOTIVATING ENERGY, capable of causing the greatest and best transformations within us, producing great achievements.

Now:

- What do you want?

- What do you dream about?

- What do you desire?

- What have you planned?

- What is your life purpose?

- What is your next goal?

- What do you really want to BE and not just HAVE, but BE?

- ❖ Be it in the conquest of TRUE LOVE, in MARRIAGE, in the construction of a FAMILY, in a new BUSINESS, in PROFESSIONAL, POLITICAL or

SOCIAL LIFE, in RELATIONSHIPS, in your DAY-TO-DAY, in that PRIVATE MOMENT "where no one sees you," BEFORE ALL AND ANY CIRCUMSTANCES, WHAT DO YOU REALLY WANT TO BE?

❖ Have you really stopped to think, HOW DO YOU WANT TO BE, TO LIVE TRULY AND NOT JUST SURVIVE?

❖ Everyone's answers to these questions are summed up in one: We just want HAPPINESS!

❖ Before taking the next steps, <u>we have to take our LOVING GOD's powerful attitude in Spirit and Truth.</u>

To EXERCISE SELF-ESTEEM and its STRENGTH, we all must consolidate this principle so that we can truly LOVE, with all intensity and make the POWER of LOVE in us infect everyone and everything.

Imagine how far we can go and the possibilities we would achieve if we take advantage of 100% (one hundred percent) of the fullness of our FREEDOM, EXERCISING THE STRENGTH OF SELF-ESTEEM, at this time, in this LIFE.

❖ **SELF-ESTEEM is SELF-LOVE! +++**

We can also call a **great quality** or virtue, belonging exclusively and individually to each one of us who decided to awaken it.

❖ It gives birth and generates SELF-CONFIDENCE, which is the ability to trust ourselves, in what we are able to accomplish, without doubting our integrity, honor and dignity.

❖ When we exercise SELF-ESTEEM, we respect ourselves and others, in defense of what is fair, in the act of promoting what is good. In what is perfect and pleasant to live in our environment, radiating "light" wherever we are. From the community and society that we live, study, work, and have fun, even in the places we pass, and so on during all our days on the incredible journey of life.

It is impressive, and at the same time surprising, to see how we are motivated and empowered by it even in "embracing" with great strength and intensity the noblest and challenging causes of life, with an emphasis on those of social and community origin, for the benefit of those who need help most.

❖ SELF-ESTEEM is the best awakening power in each of us.

❖ *It also makes the "HERO" that exists in us come to life!*

❖ By exercising SELF-ESTEEM in our lives, we are also encouraged to immerse ourselves within our own Soul, within our own Spirit, within our own Mind, our Emotions, within our entire BEING. Which is the interesting journey we must take in search of SELF-KNOWLEDGE.

Let's examine our thoughts and attitudes, identifying, in a balanced way, what are our limits, strengths and weaknesses, our qualities, and our defects. So, that we may discover a healthy way, gradually correct what is necessary for their own behavior, being gradually perfected, with all awareness, peace, and tranquility. Which will certainly lead us to achieve excellent results, even to overcome the limits we had before, propelling us with much more strength "upwards and forwards." So that from now on, and throughout the path we take towards success, in the realization of our plans and dreams that at one time seemed impossible to us, we will achieve them victoriously.

❖ **SELF-ESTEEM** is directly linked to **COURAGE** that gives us the attitude of having **FAITH, HOPE,** and **LOVE!**

SELF-DEFENSE can prevent us from falling into traps from choosing what is wrong, choosing what is worse for our lives. Because at this point, we have already learned SELF-ESTIMATE helps us identify and seek what is best for us, and not stop until we reach that goal.

Another essential point is that it also teaches us to maintain and preserve everything we have achieved. Simply, because it is good and does good; because it is healthy; because we must always value to preserve!

In doing so, we soon learn how important it is to be a blessing from GOD wherever we go in this life. To build our family, to which we dedicate and love so much, and the friends of the faith as well as those who are close to us, within our reach and also to those who relate in some positive way to each of us along the way.

A fantastic effect is that from this moment on, certainly everyone who has contact with us can be impacted by this strong and life-inspiring, edifying energy that flows from within each of us, who have already learned to exercise SELF-ESTEEM.

Experience this power that attracts all that is good, and you will be amazed at the results!

❖ SELF-ESTEEM is so incredible that it gives those who live with it the POWER of ATTRACTION of EVERYTHING GOOD, PERFECT AND NICE. This immense POWER is fundamental for us to develop with excellence, the ability to attract everything we need. So much so that we seek to exercise a full, abundant, and exceptionally successful life.

❖ In short: SELF-ESTEEM is such a vital STRENGTH that it ATTRACTS all kinds of PROSPERITY that each one of us works so hard to achieve.

EXERCISING SELF-ESTEEM everything in the UNIVERSE OF GOD starts to conspire in our favor, in such a way that it even surprises us. It is at those moments when we need it most, right after we have done everything we could do to reach a certain goal or objective. It raises us to overcome from small to great challenges, which would be totally impossible for us to overcome without it.

It is really "supernatural" how every transformation and everything that SELF-ESTEEM is capable of doing in us.

May there always be SELF-ESTEEM in our life. This living and DIVINE force within each one of us, motivates and drives us to create, conquer, and materialize our dreams, goals, and plans to live the best of this life.

EXERCISING THE STRENGTH OF SELF-ESTEEM:

☐ **We preserve our LIVES!**

☐ **Our entire Immune System is much stronger;**

☐ **We prevent and immunize ourselves against diseases;**

- ☐ **<u>We fight and overcome oppression, depression, and even the traits that causes suicide;</u>**

- ☐ **WE RECEIVE THE HEALING <u>of Spirit, Soul, and Body, strengthening our Mind.</u>**

- ☐ **We are rejuvenated and become healthier and happier!**

- ❖ *It allows us to safely arrive at a fantastic point on this path that we have traveled, through the "Beautiful Flowery Path," in search of the knowledge that comes with **INSPIRATION!***

Now, to "crown" and to establish SELF-ESTEEM within us, as the inseparable part of our behavior, we introduce you to a "great friend," **INSPIRATION**:

- ☐ INSPIRATION is a "breath" of GOD'S WISDOM. A spark of YOUR POWER "breathed" into our Spirit, which infects and strengthens our Soul, reaches and empowers our Mind, feeding our thoughts with constructive, positive, productive, and creative attitudes, it presents in our conquests.

☐ INSPIRATION is only alive and powerful in the lives of those who have SELF-ESTEEM. Those who love and value themselves are naturally kind, capable of truly loving life and all the good things it has.

☐ INSPIRATION EXERCISED WITH THE STRENGTH OF SELF-ESTEEM can make us PROSPEROUS at all levels of life until we reach the absence of needs in the sense of difficulties, which really is the PROSPERITY OF TRUTH.

Now, exercising SELF-ESTEEM, we can affirm that the TRUTH frees us and always prevails. It is everything that can never be annulled, erased, or forgotten.

Thinking in this way, we will never forget that inside each one of us, there inhabits an Excellent Spirit, a Winning Spirit, a seed that can germinate and bear fruit at the right time. It is capable of changing our lives forever and for the better, and this powerful seed is the spark of GOD!

Always remember who you are; believe in the one who created you, believe in your ability to make your dreams come true, plan, work with dedication, motivation, inspiration, and the strength of AUTOESTIMA to win.

Never forget that with GOD, all good things are possible for us!

Chapter 4

* BREAKING THROUGH THE "STORM" *

What do you feel when you look at storms, challenges, and difficulties?

Just imagine a big hurricane, a big storm, where all human beings either do not seek shelter on land or in water. Both the beings that inhabit the dry land and the beings that inhabit the waters, when the great storm is approaching, flee in search of shelter. However, as the legend says, except for this animal:

AN EAGLE!

The EAGLE senses that a storm is coming, IT flies against the storm, straight into the center of the storm and crosses the storm, breaking through the storm!

Even though it knows that it is risking its life, because of the immense concentration of energy inside a storm, but IT doesn't panic, IT doesn't stay in place nor flee away. The noise that scares everyone, made by a storm,does not paralyze an EAGLE. It does not chase it away, it does not frighten it, it does not cause panic, it does not cause terror in an EAGLE. On the contrary, it motivates it to face it, it defies the storm.

In an attitude of great strength and courage, IT aims at the center of it and breaks through the storm!

Faster than the "wind."

Do you know why?

Because IT knows that by breaking the storm, IT will have overcome it, and will have its reward. A tremendous view of the "blue infinite," the wonderful SKY that awaits her, "drizzled or showered" with stars, IT will find the Moon and all the splendor of the magnificent Sun!

In the midst of a stormy moment, a tremendous sight that only inside an aircraft, perhaps the human being can glimpse. However, not even the most powerful aircraft can break a big storm, as an EAGLE DOES.

Because the EAGLE has SELF-ESTEEM!

THE EAGLE is of extraordinary COURAGE!

IT discovers early on that HOPE WINS FEAR!

IT learned to DEFEAT anxiety in any and all circumstances during its life. IT is abundant in patience! When it's time to hunt, IT is in no hurry because it has overcome all anxiety. It knows very well how to wait for the best time to capture its prey.

IT learned to EARN its SELF DOMAIN;

IT learned to EXERCISE THE STRENGTH OF SELF-ESTEEM;

Then, as we saw, IT BREAKS the storm and finds the BEAUTIFUL SKY!

THE BEAUTIFUL HEAVEN!

THE SUN!

THE MOON and the STARS!

IT contemplates it all!

Because, if it's daytime, IT sees the BLUE SKY, above the storm, which is beautiful, it's tremendous!

And it sees the SUN with its extreme brightness, at its maximum strength, that only those above the storm can see.

And, if it's at night, IT has a "bonus."

IT has the "special something..."

IT can see, beyond the SUN, THE MOON, and the STARS!

* Think about it, because to overcome life's adversities, we have to break the storm.

☐ After all, what does a storm represent in everyone's life?

☐ What is your storm?

☐ What prevents you from winning, from overcoming, going forward, reaching, and obtaining your victory?

☐ What keeps you from prospering?

☐ What is your biggest difficulty?

☐ What is your biggest challenge?

☐ How big is the storm over your life today?

Pay attention, aim at the target, stay firm, keep your mind focused on planning. As we just suggested in the previous chapter, take Faith's attitude, and have a conversation with GOD. Ask for His guidance, experience a deep peace, obey his guidance, focus on the effectiveness of his teachings and live with the fullness of His Commandments. So that you will achieve an excellent quality of life, which you never dreamed of or even imagined.

When we "walk" with GOD, everything in our lives changes radically. We are surprised by His new day-by-day, step by step, confirming through new experiences that we will have with His presence, that we are truly born again and that we will never be like that before we have this extraordinary intimacy with Him!

One of the good and opportune examples of this dimension of relationship with GOD, which also motivates us to go much further in these Divine precepts, is how HE Speaks to King David. He speaks with the "breath of inspiration" contained in His Word that is recorded in the Ancient Testament of the Bible, specifically in Psalm 32, in verse 08:

"The Lord says, I will instruct you and guide you in the way to follow; my eyes will be on you to advise you."

Believe and reflect that the great strength of this promise is also there to build your life.

Now, with all the conviction present in our Faith, we declare that after receiving from God, the power contained in these eternal words, we will certainly experience a fantastic supernatural portion of His Infinite Wisdom as we act according to His guidance. And then:

☐ We will be clothed with the greatest and strongest celestial armor;

☐ We will be molded after the "heart of GOD;"

☐ With what is most powerful;

- ☐ Equipped with our best weaponry, we will set out with all courage and patience to overcome and surpass all limits, until today was impossible for us to overcome.

Today, let's look at the center of the "storm," asking GOD to give us the "Vision of His Holy Spirit" to win!

And, also, here in the figurative sense, a vision similar to that of an EAGLE, and his courage to BREAK the whole storm!

- ☐ We have to apply all discipline and intelligence to know the right time to attack and the right time to defend ourselves.

- ☐ We need to know the right time to act and the right time to not act and wait.

- ☐ We need to wait for the right moment, for the exact time to make the correct calculation, to STOP the storms that are over our lives, with the same efficiency as an EAGLE BREAKS its storms!

☐ Because we cannot be careless;

☐ Because if we are careless, we will certainly be defeated.

☐ However, if we are as cautious as an EAGLE, WE WIN!

BY "aiming at our targets, in the different storms of life," we will have the patience and the firmness of the spirit to reach the "hurricane eye" and break it efficiently, at the precise time, in the right way and without anxiety.

HOPE OVERCOMES FEAR because we are...

☐ DEFEATING ANXIETY!

☐ GAINING OUR SELF DOMAIN!

☐ EXERCISING THE STRENGTH OF SELF-ESTEEM!

We can never forget those principles that make us prosper and win.

How about we now "travel in time," quickly and for a moment into the past, when our ancestors lived?

We must remember that, since ancient times, humanity has been challenged to face and weather storms so that they may go further to develop and prosper.

It is not different from our ancestors, it is no different with each one of us, and "it certainly will not be different with our descendants, because everyone somehow faces storms in life. But, to face a storm:

☐ We have to have courage!

☐ A well-designed flight plan; strong and powerful like the flight of an EAGLE!

☐ We need to have "GOD'S VISION" just as the one he gave the eagle!

We need to put on "COURAGE and FAITH; STRENGTH; of the INVINCIBLE ARMOR

OF GOD, with all His ARMAMENT," and manage everything with His WISDOM, so that not even a damage, we will suffer. Like an EAGLE when the storm breaks.

Although the roar of the storm always demonstrates its "terror," with great bang and enormous size, threatening to annihilate everything and everyone in its path, an EAGLE is not intimidated. It does not believe in such a threat, quite the opposite, IT FACES; IT BREAKS THROUGH, and IT WINS the "terror" caused by a storm!

We cannot fail to open a space here "on this journey" to register a solemn event, which changed our days, and the way we lived, deprived our freedom and the history of humanity.

As everyone may know, it is also a difficult "episode," a time in our lives when we all suffer a "cowardly surprise attack from an unusual enemy." We had to get up to react and strike back quickly. Fighting with faith, courage, and strength, this unprecedented cruel and unknown threat to freedom, which silently attacked China in Wuhan City first, having been reported to the world for the first time in September 2019.

Its scientific and epidemiological name is Covid19, the most Infectious, Viral, and Deadly Pandemic of recent times, so fast that it quickly covered our planet, devastating, contaminating, and killing multitudes. Pushing humanity into a huge global crisis!

This is the "battle" for all of us!

The moment when we need to unite, even more, exercising compassion and mercy, praying for one another, asking in faith for the help of GOD, believing in His LOVE Agape, His Eternal WISDOM, and His Great POWER! Because HE IS THE ONLY CAPABLE OF SAVING everyone. Whether through a miracle, a strong deliverance, or even "pouring out" Your Inspiration, the wisdom, Intelligence, and Creativity, with all Direction for the Development of REMEDY that CURE and VACCINE that IMMUNIZES. Only then will it be possible to ROMPER this "storm," much faster, efficiently, and with less damage, to actually WIN the Covid pandemic19.

Unfortunately, we know that many of our brothers and sisters have already fallen and will still fall in the middle of the road " because there are millions of infected and more than half a million dead. However, in this "battle," too, there are many more winners: we count millions who have been and continue to be cured, in addition to those who form the vast majority of the world population that exceeds 7.7 billion, who have not even been contaminated, until now, by the virus Covid19, the cause of this pandemic.

Without losing focus, my family and I took advantage of the excellent opportunity to register here, in a very personal way, in total unity, with all the conviction and faith, which we sincerely believe, without doubt, that all our "brothers and sisters who fall," When they close their eyes here on Earth," they will return home "and open them immediately in Heaven, where they will be with GOD, in Glory!

Dwelling in the Eternal Kingdom that has been prepared for us since the beginning of Creation! So, whatever the outcome of this "battle," we have already won the "War" because death has no more power over us !!!

In this way, we understand that everything we go through in this life contributes to our improvement.

Also, we believe in the Word of God, which is in the New Testament, in the Christian Bible, in the Letter of the Apostle Paul to the Romans, in chapter 08, of verse 28, saying:

"And we know that all things God works for the good of those who love him, who have been called according to his purpose."

- We believe that when we focus on the "target," our adversities, challenges, and the "storms" of this world do not deter-mine who we are.

- What determines who we are is how we react to difficulties.

- In the face of tribulations and great storms that threaten our lives.

- It's what defines us.

- It is what determines us and tells us who we are and who we belong to.

And as we preserve that conscience alive in our spirit, we know that we are children of GOD!

Therefore, we are no longer "afraid" of death because we have already overcome it!

- ☐ As it is written in the Letter of the Apostle Paul to the Romans, in chapter 08, of verse 35:

"Who shall separate us from the love of Christ? Shall trouble or hardship or persecution or famine or nakedness or danger or sword?"

Chapter 5

THE ILLUMINATING SUN

Imagine waking up to a beautiful sunny spring weekend morning, and you can leisurely walk freely in green fields, smell the flowers, the gardens, and fruit trees. The refreshing breeze carries with it an infinity of natural perfumes, a strong sense of peace and harmony, amid the free birds singing!

In this "magical" moment, well beyond the tops of the tallest trees, you look at the majestic sky, without any apparent cloud, and see the sun illuminating the blue immensity, within that fertile season, where life is restored all around you!

It's a fantastic and extraordinary phenomenon, the force of nature that renews life, isn't it?

This same phenomenon must occur within each one of us, passing through our spirit, traveling through our soul, our body, and reviving our mind. Providing us with a great renewal, with a "vision" much further than we could see before, bringing to our reality the dimension of a "new horizon," where true prosperity and its essence, called simplicity, live!

It is remarkable how the rare beauty majestically rests on everything simple!

Gradually revealing something surprising, so delicate and at the same time so strong.

And the most fantastic thing to discover and understand is that true prosperity is revealed in simplicity!

And it is simply what gives us balance, security, achievement, comfort, and full peace, within the realization of our most incredible goals, dreams, and plans.

How many solutions throughout the human development process of most incredible inventions have been materialized through simplicity?

Because in doing so, we are much happier, we feel truly fulfilled. That consists of the ability to have harmony and only seek for what is perfect and necessary for our lives: without exaggeration, without greed, without pride, without envy, and the deception of human vanities!

Therefore, we will dominate everything we own instead of being dominated by everything we have.

We will be free from the slavery that the excess of everything dominates over all who have it.

Paying attention to the small details that bring us peace and happiness, we will learn to value what really matters. Giving value to what really matters, we achieve the long-awaited quality of life, which comes from simplicity.

Because true simplicity attracts wisdom and all that is good, it makes us reach the highest places of prosperity and consolidates our success.

Being a simple person does not mean failing to enjoy the best in this world; quite the contrary, being a simple person, in addition to enjoying and possessing the best of this life, you will also be a more beautiful and much stabler person, happier and much more fulfilled at all levels of your existence.

☐ You will know what real prosperity is!

☐ This blessing will reach your life..

☐ And you will be able to progress in all the good that is in this dimension.

It is worth mentioning that financial prosperity is significant and constitutes a significant part of prosperity. However, real prosperity is much more ...

☐ PROSPERITY IS THE
   ABSENCE OF NEED!

☐ IT IS TO BE, NOT ONLY TO HAVE.

To thrive is to be simple, to be truly happy, to find beauty, peace, and harmony, starting from small things. It's radiating this "magic" in all areas and stages of life. It is a very particular way. Each of us gives priority and is focused.

Being:

- In mental, physical, and spiritual health;

- In love;

- In the family;

- In the business and professional career he chose to develop;

- Free, balanced, accomplished, conscious, and blissful;

- Stable emotionally and consolidated in spirit;

- A blessing in good social relationships;

- Able to do what he likes best;

- Firm and upright;

- Good generous and kind;

- Friendly and Faithful;

- Blessed and walking with God on this life journey and beyond.

Let there be the power of the simplicity of truth in our lives, every day and wherever we go. That may accomplish everything we dream of and have a life with quality and abundance. May we be reached by the luck that comes from GOD that restores, builds, and prospers all who are simple in heart. Giving them the absence of needs and having perfect peace!

It is essential to keep the flame of FAITH, HOPE, and LOVE, well lit in our hearts. To never forget the importance of celebrating the spectacular Divine Gift of life, the greatest blessing that we could receive, and that GOD gave us for free.

Let us see and be inspired by the Word of God, spoken by JESUS CHRIST, which is written in the New Testament, within the Gospel, recorded by the Apostle Matthew, in chapter 6, verse 22:

"The eye is the lamp of the body. If your eyes are healthy, your whole body will be full of light."

- ☐ Those who have a simple life live more and in peace. They have learned not to complicate things, making their day-to-day goals as simple as possible.

They discover that by paying attention to details and fixing your gaze on what is easy, on what is benign, and on what matters most deviates you completely from evil and closing your eyes to everything that is not good. You find simplicity and are surprised by it! And so, you really manage to see that it is there that the greatest meaning of life lives, where true happiness lives. That is what is waiting for each one of us!

- ☐ So, let's not think of negative things because we are born of light. We well know that wherever our eyes are looking, there will also be our spirit, emotions, and "heart."

- ☐ Focus your gaze on everything pure and innocent, because innocence is the absence of guilt, and there is no evil in it!

- ❖ **<u>The brilliance of the sun will brighten our eyes, and our whole being will be illuminated, and we will overcome the darkness of this world!</u>**

Chapter 6

TAKING A LEAP OF FAITH

Certainly, there are several definitions and practical meanings of the word FAITH. They have impacted us and caused incredible changes in humankind's history since the beginning of creation.

In our understanding:

❖ **"FAITH IS THE GREATEST ATTRACTION POWER OF THOUGHT THAT BRINGS EXISTENCE EVERYTHING**

THAT WE TRULY BELIEVE AND NEED IT TO BE MATERIALIZED IN THE DIMENSION AS IF IT ALREADY EXISTED!"

Now, right now, think about your big goal!

Think of your most extraordinary dream!

On your biggest plans!

What you need most!

What is practically impossible to achieve!

In what after having done everything, you still have not managed to accomplish!

For your healing or for those who need it most!

In the great deliverance, whatever it may be!

In a supernatural MIRACLE !!!

Look up, take a deep breath, and imagine:

☐ There's nothing impossible for God!

☐ With God, everything is possible for us!

What is missing to bring your greatest dream into existence, as if it already existed?

❖ TAKE A LEAP OF FAITH!

❖ LIVE WITH SELF-ESTEEM!

❖ STRATEGIZE*

❖ STAY FOCUSED*

❖ SELF-DISCIPLINE*

❖ SUBMIT ALL YOUR PLANS TO GOD.

❖ REST*

❖ BE PATIENT*

❖ CAST OFF ALL ANXIETY.

❖ EARN YOUR SELF DOMAIN AND BE IN CONTROL OF THE SITUATION, YOUR EMOTIONS, YOUR THOUGHTS; YES, BELIEVE WITH ALL boldness and INTREPIDITY.

❖ BE COURAGEOUS!

❖ BREAK THROUGH THE "STORM!"

❖ ENJOY THE ILLUMINATING SUN!

❖ FOCUS ON SOLUTIONS NOT DIFFICULTIES*

❖ ***EXERCISE INTELLIGENT FAITH, THE ONE THAT TAKES ALL THE POWER OF THOUGHT***

And what is FAITH if not the firm purpose, and the strong foundation of believing in the things that are invisible to us. It's everything we hope for, without even doubting for a moment of everything we believe, without doubt, so that such things become visible to us?

The certainty of FAITH is built with a real attitude of believing!

And FAITH brings into existence the power of GOD in our lives and keeps within us the greatest and most powerful SELF-ESTEEM.

And from there, with your SELF-ESTEEM strengthened by GOD, in a supernatural way, take possession of the impossible, of the invisible power that together with FAITH brings the existence of your dreams, as if they already existed.

What is most important in your life?

In your day-to-day?

Are you, am I , are we all, dreaming and wishing what is best for us?

And is what we think is the best for us, also the best for those who are with us, from our family to everyone around us?

Have you stopped to think about it?

Have you thought about God's greatness, the Creator of all things visible and invisible?

Have you reflected on the immensity of His Love for all of us and how merciful is HE?

Can our mind fathom the dimension of GOD? So, why doubt?

Using our FAITH to build and prosper at all levels in life, it's fitting to simultaneously pay close attention to everything that happens around us and the "signs of the times." This helps us to be able to reflect effectively on things that have happened till now and what will happen until the very end. As prophesied by our ancestors and "Heroes of the Faith" in the Book of Revelation in the New Testament BIBLE, that "THE END" will bring a new beginning for the sons and daughters of GOD!

We are living in times of war and rumors of war. Times of conflict and violence "everywhere and all over the world." Times of increasingly strong natural catastrophes: Fires, Earthquakes, Tsunamis, Storms, Hurricanes, Tornadoes, Great Rains and their Floods and much more that both destroy and kill.

In times of terrible pests and epidemics, and even an unprecedented pandemic, such as the one of the Covid19 Virus, infecting millions and killing thousands of people in our generation, "devastating the earth," as we said earlier, in Chapter 4 - BREAKING the storm.

Times of critical Global Crisis!

Times of growing injustice, murders of innocents, and all kinds of inequality and violence.

We are living in a time when there is a lot of misery, there is a lot of hunger, there is a lot of want in the midst of humanity, where the majority lack everything and there is no resources.

So, where should we really put our attention and FAITH to resist and fight such things at this time?

What are we really doing to change this "tribulation," this sad situation, which is moving fast to soon become a global "tribulation?"

And what can we do together to change this state of great confusion that affects, harms, and threatens our freedom?

We feel that it is necessary to "walk with GOD." We have Love, Unity, Faith, and Courage to work together with all Hope until we see our "Earth Healed."

Let's take a LEAP OF FAITH. Begin this process within yourself, your family, and in your social life and friends. Encourage everyone to do the same until they manage to gather and consolidate their entire community in a single purpose of Peace!

Share the vision of preserving peace with everyone within your reach. Only in this way, you will begin forming a movement of harmony and unity, atmosphere of love, balance, equality, and justice. Flourish with all the fraternity that will radiate and cause the necessary transformations within each of us so that there is a more just and humane society!

Do you realize how FAITH can be a powerful, positive instrument capable of producing all kinds of changes in your life, in the environment in which we live, and in the history of all of us?

Remember to dedicate the fruits of FAITH and LOVE, with COMPASSION and MERCY!

Chapter 7

LIVING WITH COURAGE

<u>Receiving life is a fantastic and an extraordinary thing!</u>

And before we even receive it, there must be an act of great courage, to beat a multitude of others to it.

A tiny and microscopic particle that forms us needs to be the first to fertilize the egg so that there is an explosion of life !!!

We are here on this incredible planet that we have learned to call Earth!

Living with courage in this beautiful journey that is LIFE!

So, What is courage?

Each one may have their own definition that helps better understand the meaning of courage.

However, I have my own personal way of describing what courage means. It's A COURAGEOUS ATTITUDE TO FACE AND OVERCOME OUR FEARS!

That COURAGE that descends from SELF-ESTEEM also pushes us up and forward!

Instead of running away, we run towards what most afflicts us.

It is often an "instinctive" attitude.

At other times, it is a "calculated" attitude for those who, from a certain moment on, learned to handle with care and balance the power of COURAGE, reaching perfection, overcoming adversity in various circumstances, until they reached your goals and plans.

Therefore, COURAGE should not be used in any which way, any time, for any reason. Because within COURAGE, there is the honor that motivates us to defend what is righteous; to defend an innocent: Be a friend, a relative, or a stranger simply; that "noble" cause and worth defending.

It is the strength and instinct that moves us to save a son or daughter!

The natural and uncontrollable urge to protect our great love, our family, and those we love the most!

It takes a lot of COURAGE to really LOVE!

Courage is well known for the immense power to defend ourselves from the dangers sur-rounding us and even the unexpected.

How much COURAGE do we need to declare our LOVE to someone?

COURAGE to say yes to what is good, and COURAGE to say no to what is evil.

COURAGE makes us keep the "flames" of SELF-DISCIPLINE, SELF DOMAIN, and SELF-ESTEEM, always burning inside us, obeying our conscience resist the temptations of vanities, which we may fall into.

Since the beginning, ACTS of COURAGE have marked the history of humankind:

☐ Liberating!

☐ Preserving!

☐ Defending!

☐ Protecting!

Courageous people that...

* ❖ Created Civilizations!

* ❖ Liberated people from slavery!

* ❖ Constructed, unified and established nations!

* ❖ Discovered and invented all technology that molded our society!

* ❖ Dominated the Earth, Sea and Space!

* ❖ They never gave up!

* ❖ They persist and go beyond, exceeding all expectations, in search of conquering the "impossible."

* ❖ They create and discover, more and more, new technologies that make us take a leap in knowledge and quality of life.

❖ Leading, fighting, and winning together, and for one purpose, to declare independence!

❖ They wrote the real Constitution.

❖ They implemented a strong and lasting democracy.

❖ They raised the Freedom Flag at the highest point!

An attitude of COURAGE is something tremendous. It changes everything. It preserves life, inspires us, and drives us to overcome the most difficult challenges. It helps overcome the greatest obstacles, the tests of this world. The tests that we are subjected to at all times and that is to overcome the "fierce" dispute that always exists in our society to achieve a better position in this life. To and even in the "struggle" for survival, amid the great difficulties that suddenly appear before us.

As we said, from the beginning, the "battle for life" continues with courage. It does not stop, and it starts well before we are born. For our life to be formed, an event of courage must happen.

Let's reflect on this for a moment:

What is scariest and more frightening to you?

What ails you the most?

What scares you and makes you step back or think about stepping back and even running away?

What causes such things?

Certainly, if we stop to think, in a very particular and special way, each of us will identify what really scares us, causes fear, afflicts, and often makes us run away.

Thankfully, in time we will find the answers. Our understanding opens new horizons providing us with an extraordinary view of the dimension in which we live.

In this "journey called life," challenging surprises arise. We are provoked at all times to take action. It is at this time that we have to remember certain important lessons.

Now, before taking the first step, in any direction, whether to the right or left, descending or ascending, it is necessary to observe the environment in which you are, right?

This is exactly how it should be at all times when you have to make a decision or make a choice. Remember that before reacting or responding to a certain situation that requires courage, even in an emergency, where you will have very little time to act, even if instinctively, you will have to quickly assess and master the entire situation in which you are inserted so that you may efficiently overcome the circumstance with courage.

It is worthwhile to go a little deeper into the extraordinary process that occurs at birth:

After fertilization, that "magical" explosive moment, when the egg is fertilized and begins the creation of life, inside the maternal womb, there is an incredible gestation period in which human life takes shape, grows, and develops. When the time comes for the baby to be born, which traditionally lasts for 9 months, except for premature births, where these gestational periods vary mostly between 06, 07, or 08 months, a phenomena is registered more and more recurring today.

The creation of life is unpredictable and independent of the specialists' willingness to participate.

It, LIFE, is independent of this world!

Life, in my point of view, is "supernatural." And its essence continues to surprise all science.

Observing how life is formed we can witness its greatness and the act of sovereignty that exists at all times of its creation. Without forgetting to analyze every fantastic process that precedes creation itself. All of this and every detail of this "magic" formation shows us that life is really "supernatural".

Imagine how much courage a mother must have to have a developing life within her!

The care she has, right after this great act of love, and courage is consummated.

The incomparable experience of a woman in her first pregnancy and the extraordinary path she will have to travel until the day of her first child birth!

Try to imagine the immense expectation and the whirlwind of emotions experienced by a mother, from fertilization, throughout pregnancy, until the long awaited time of delivery!

What about the surprising journey into the unknown of childbirth for parents?

They wonder how it will be?

They try to imagine this near future and the surprises it will bring. That's how all of us, passionate about life, behave in a situation like this.

No matter how much they have advised, read, heard, watched, and studied about motherhood and fatherhood. Everything is very new, incredibly challenging, and exciting. To have a complete, safe, happy, and healthy family after this extraordinary moment and share the good news of a baby's arrival. Everything changes, and it will certainly not be the same as before. Nothing can stop the shocking surprise and fully prepare us for this great novelty, strong emotion, fulfillment, and happiness, which comes with a child's birth!

It is an extraordinary experience for parents, their families, doctors, nurses, and other health professionals involved in the birth of the new human life. However, no one can comprehend what a woman feels when giving birth to a child! Nothing compares to the "unique and exclusive" experience. It is unique, and personal courage is only found in a mother's courage.

It is through a new life that we are brought to the dimension of our existence! This tiny life is already faced with the challenge of being born and survives because of its act of great courage to do its part. But the more fragile baby needs to "fight" and do his part with his mother.

It is magnificent to see all this "magic."

What a charming discovery this little human being makes!

Let's keep going with this...

When a baby is born, it needs to have the courage to open its eyes. It makes an extra effort before or simultaneously and manages to breathe independently in our atmosphere outside from its mother's body, fully using its survival instinct.

When it realizes the newness of life out here, a new and surprising dimension, it continues with courage until unfamiliar hands place it in the arms of someone he knows deep within itself, its mother. It then snuggles in her arms and quickly feels safe, and soon calms down.

See how much courage for the birth of a new human life was needed to enter this fantastic and extraordinary world.

What a charming discovery this little human being makes!

To discover life, this fragile, helpless baby is so dependent on his parents' courage and love to raise him with all the care, provision, good education, and security.

With its pure survival instinct, and through the motivation and protection its parents give it, in addition to those who care for it, it keeps adapting and learning gradually. He learns to face and overcome anxiety and fear in a very peculiar, extraordinary, precious, and inspiring way.

The baby continues its "journey" of discoveries towards the unknown with great courage. It launches itself to overcome and break the challenges that are gradually appearing before it.

It will face many new obstacles and limits that it will have to overcome every day. It will experience a new phase of its life towards development, starting with:

☐ Learning to communicate when it's thirsty or hungry, needs a diaper change, or that it's in pain and feeling some discomfort. Expressing restlessness and wants to be held to feel safe on its parents' lap and everything else it may need. To achieve that, it will naturally use its most basic instincts, using the only form of communication it knows. Its emotions are expressed in an exceptional way that babies discern how to use very well and much better than everyone else. He smiles, signaling that he is happy, emitting several magnificent, peculiar, and exclusive sounds that only babies are capable of making; it also tries to get its parents' attention for a need needing to be met at that moment and then that cycle is repeated.

☐ It is challenging to get around and learn to move from laying face down to the one position it is used to most of the time, face up. Until this moment, when he gains more confidence until he can turn and roll from side to side, trying a little more day-to-day. It learns to practice sitting and gets firmer by facing more and more gravity and its body's weight. It starts to "crawl" and goes a little further every day until it can stand up. It falls and gets up, over and over again. It perseveres, in its own way and with the help of its parents, until finally overcoming the biggest challenge to stay upright. Then, it takes the next steps, and so on. Always proceeding with great courage. It grows and develops, facing, adapting, supporting, and overcoming everything. It learns to overcome adversities in the midst of many changes, which occur in a tremendous sequence in its challenging and lovely life!

☐ To improve its communication and to relate, more and more, with other people, besides its parents, family, other relatives and friends who are part of its most intimate circle. For example; When its parents take it to medical appointments, it faces the new surprises with great courage!

☐ Who is that stranger?...

☐ It is confronted and sometimes cries, is reluctant, is encouraged, and soon adapts to the situation. Strangers' hands examine it, and then, on the way home, he observes the surroundings, other people, the landscapes, and everything on earth and the sky. Finally, when it gets home, it goes to practice walking again at the first opportunity it has. It faces the risk of falling, confident on its feet, it falls, and courageously gets back up again!

☐ Alone or with the help of the parents, this exercise is repeated every day, until it gains firmness in its steps.

☐ Then comes that moment its parents have to take it to experience another environment, a little further than the usual one when they take it to the experience of walking in a beautiful garden and feeling the grass between its toes.

• I speak from experience because I observed closely and participated in this process by my wife's side, raising our daughter, the courageous Victoria, printing her first footprints on the earth.

How fantastic is this incredible journey!

I remember it as if it were yesterday. The courage she possessed to set foot in the front yard of the apartment we lived in. She made one step and got a little scared, then she felt confident and motivated by us. She put the second foot on, steadied herself, and then started walking slowly, holding our hands. With each step, she gained a little more speed. She let go of our hands and walked beside us, when suddenly, she fell sitting down, looked at us, paused, pushed herself up, and continued walking, falling and rising, gaining more and more self-confidence. It was perfected taking walks in both the gardens and the sand on the beaches, where she left her small footprints in life!

These small and "magical" moments are the ones that most move us, inspire us, and mark our history tremendously. We learned from this that it is necessary to have extreme courage so that we will rise when we fall.

It is truly incredible, fantastic, and extraordinary to see the immense power of courage in our lives' essence, through the innocent speculation that makes us reach knowledge with the strong emotion of the experience lived by a child!

How tremendous we can witness the magnitude and nature of this reality! The unsurpassed strength that is in the Genesis of us all!

And there is no stopping, quite the contrary; we continue to develop constantly. Being continually perfected, radiating this immense power, with great boldness, to everything within our reach, within the immense dimension of this life! After all, I believe in a very personal way that courage is a power that we received to live with, even before we were born in this dimension.

We have the greatest improvement in this challenging life that, being so, will impel us to go much further than we can imagine.

After all, we are much more than we dream of being or have the capacity to understand!

❖ **We have FAITH that the exceptional event that causes the explosion of life is the greatest proof of COURAGE's eternity that is also BORN OF LOVE with SELF-ESTEEM to CREATE LIFE itself!**

Chapter 8

MAKING SACRIFICES

SACRIFICE!

SACRIFICE IS A STRONG WORD;

IT'S AN ANCIENT WORD;

IT'S A POWERFUL WORD;

IT IS A WORD THAT BROUGHT INTO
EXISTENCE SALVATION. AND IT WAS
EXACTLY THAT ATTITUDE WRAPPED
WITH LOVE, FAITH AND HOPE THAT

MAKES US OVERCOME DEATH TO ENTER INTO ETERNAL LIFE. for THROUGH THIS GREATEST ACT OF LOVE FOR HUMANKIND, THE ETERNAL LIVING GOD, GAVE US ETERNAL LIFE THROUGH THE REVELATION OF HIS SON JESUS CHRIST.

In this way, we can say that SACRIFICE is a LOVE, FAITH, and HOPE attitude.

SACRIFICE also means to renounce what is most important, IN THE PURPOSE OF PROMOTING A GREATER GOOD.

Our authentic prosperity must be reborn so that we may perform the sacrifice to kill our vanities.

There are many types and forms, different levels, various motives, and purposes of SACRIFICES.

We believe that in special circumstances, in the search for the extraordinary, without SACRIFICE, THERE IS NO VICTORY!

Then, examine yourself to see if there is any-thing you need to sacrifice to achieve a greater good, a bigger goal, a greater meaning for your life (your existence).

How many times do we have the chance to prosper, but because of all the distraction or dedicating ourselves to what has no importance we lose focus and time, we are kept from expe-riencing this "magical" place. Where can we find this place?

Only after we have lost such an opportunity do we realize that we have missed the great chance for success in our lives?

If we don't watch and stay focused on what we want, we get distracted, and the great chance of accomplishment passes right before our eyes without even realizing it.

We often fail to see what really matters and can't see what is actually happening in each of lives' circumstances.

However, if we stop and pay close attention, we will certainly see that luck, chances, and opportunities exist to favor those who believe and strive.

Knowing that at the right time, we will reach them. If everyone does their part and remains firmly in the right place, after having done everything in their power; having, above all, a good purpose, patience, and acting with intelligence, discipline, planning, dedication, concentration, and the incredible power of thought, faith, courage and SACRIFICE.

Similarly, our ancestors prevailed and left us these and other teachings as a great legacy of their trajectory recorded in the numerous books that portray humankind's history.

Before each inspired sacrifice that we are inspired and encouraged to make throughout life, it is necessary to examine with common sense and conscience to obtain a complete view of all the circumstances surrounding the situation and make sure we are in the right place.

The right way is adopting the right and most appropriate attitude to achieve our goals with the highest use rate that consolidates all success.

The greater our level of obedience to the immutable principles and rules present in the virtue known as integrity, the greater will be our victory and the consequent prosperity.

We must never make sacrifices in vain, where there is no honor and integrity from start to finish.

Wisdom must shape our behavior by being inseparable from our thoughts, our intentions, and all the actions we take.

Imagine a moment when we are faced with an urgency of having to save the life of an unknown person, such as:

We have to donate our blood to help save a person's life urgently.

Keeping the same frame of thought, let's go a little further and imagine another possibility that exists. Another significant focal point in a common circumstance that happens frequently is a well-known fact that every level of sacrifice can increase. In this case, we have to decide to donate some bone marrow. This will not be missing from our organism; to donate a small part of our liver that also regenerates, or even an organ, like one of the two kidneys we have, saves a life.

Be it one of those we love most: a wife, a husband, one of our children, those who are so precious and who are part of our sacred family; or one of our closest loved ones: a mother, a father, a brother, a sister; a niece, a nephew, an aunt, an uncle, a cousin, a cousin, a grandmother, a grandfather; or maybe a friend, a friend.

What if that person were a stranger, we know nothing about whether it is a good or bad person, where they are from, or how they have lived?

When it comes to saving the life of an unknown innocent person, especially if it's a child, it is naturally easier, or is it not?

Yes. This responsibility flows from within us in an instinctively quick and spontaneous way, correct?

So, what if this person is totally unknown to you?

Now, let's take another interesting step in this reflection:

What if you know this person but have no sympathy for them?

Can you imagine that?

Would we have enough unconditional love to make the sacrifice for this person?

Making sacrifices for ourselves and those we love is very easy. Making sacrifices for those we have no affinity with is very difficult, even more, difficult than sacrificing for those we have never seen or even heard of.

However, to overcome this challenge, behind every sacrifice we make we need this extraordinary thing called LOVE!

Because without LOVE, there is no SACRIFICE.

In this sense and objective that we are reflecting on, true SACRIFICE is mainly the attitude of renouncing what is most important to us at that moment in favor of achieving a greater good.

It was like this in our ancestors' lives, where they were faced with the need to make great SACRIFICES!

However, they did so because in them was the greatest power that is LOVE.

Whether it is self LOVE or for someone else.

Really without LOVE, there would never be SACRIFICE.

There are other reasons and attitudes of sacrifices. Even sacrificing a patrimony and a material good is necessary to have love to help our children, a relative, our parents, a friend, and other people, institutions, known or unknown to us, even when it's to sacrifice everything for the great love of our life!

A crucial point in this reflection we are making is the fact that there are many sacrifices that birth parents make for the sake of their children! These parents are endowed with a strong attitude of unconditional love.

Looking at the relationship we just registered here from another angle, we leave you with an intriguing question:

And the children, would they sacrifice with the same unconditional and true love for their parents' good?

Because everyone who truly loves, loves unconditionally!

What sacrifice have you made in your life?

What did you sacrifice for someone?

What sacrifice have you made for yourself?

It is imperative to understand that all successful journeys always begin with sacrifices necessary to achieve our lives' goals and objectives with intelligence and wisdom.

Imagine how many times in life, we encounter circumstances in which we have to make a choice. To make the right choice and achieve the goal, we need to renounce what we "like the most" to achieve something even greater on most occasions, which is sometimes far the challenge and difficulty are beyond our own understanding.

It is tough to quickly understand why we have to renounce what is "very important" to each of us to achieve something greater.

Why, that only "giving up what I like most ...", will I be able to hit the target and win?

Each of us has "fights and battles," challenges to overcome limits and obstacles that arise in our path in search of reaching our goals and objectives, that purpose, and that victory we most want to achieve.

Each one of us knows how to identify this very well in our own life. We all know, however, it isn't easy to see.

Because if it were easy, there would only be winners in the world, right? Everyone would be winners in this world!

But, this is not how things are in our super competitive society.

In fact, the circle of winners, unfortunately, is still a small one. I believe with all my heart that more and more winners are entering this circle. It will grow bigger and bigger in such a way that will open opportunities to include more and more victorious, accomplished, and happy members until this circle becomes the size of our planet. We will materialize the great dream in which all become winners and harmonious with each other.

Do you believe that if we all work with integrity in a firm purpose and do our part, our most "impossible" dreams can come true?

It is fascinating to be able to think and reflect this way.

I feel a strong sense of freedom that comes with seeing this possible realization.

How wonderful the arrival of this day will be!

It is worth taking the opportunity to remind ourselves of the importance of not being deceived and starting to pursue "delusions," working, investing our time, efforts, and resources, making sacrifices in the wrong direction, aiming at false targets pursuing goals in vain: the types that will not build our lives, anything or anyone in the long run.

And how can we achieve this level of improvement?

Exercising the discernment that we acquire with Self Domain.

Therefore, we will choose and finally dispense with "excess baggage," representing everything that we really do not need. Therefore, we also should not preserve or maintain these things in our lives. Even for many of us, this attitude can be considered an intelligent type of sacrifice, do you agree?

Especially after we reach prosperity, shouldn't we?

This is much more evident if we look at the great inequality in our society, correct?

It is essential to understand that every true sacrifice is made in a lucid, perfectly balanced, without causing harm to anyone. Because love comes before sacrifice, it does not hurt or harm anyone. On the contrary, love prefers to sacrifice itself, benefit, protect, defend, preserve, and even save lives.

When we see, become aware, and take the right attitude to sacrifice, giving up all excess in our lives, whatever nature or origin it is, we will be collaborating and entering a dimension of inner peace and harmony.

In addition to achieving our important victories, we will contribute step by step to the construction of a more just and happy society.

With this understanding, we will gain more awareness of everything important and is happening around us. Because what was obstructing our vision has been removed, and thus, what is hidden will begin to be revealed to us little by little, through new experiences acquired daily, renewing the journey of life.

We agree that there have always been, are, and will be circumstances of sacrifices in life.

There is a very relevant factor that can also influence our behavior, emotions, and consequently, our prosperity. That's kindness, a powerful virtue that must always be present in all good relationships.

This requires focus and vigilance from all of us during the process of building, defending, and maintaining a good reputation, with strong credibility, harmony, and productivity.

Such credibility is essential to the conquest and consolidation of an important and essential exclusive area of each person's life, called success.

So, this is a different sacrifice, which translates into the intelligent exercise of quickly removing from our lives what is harmful, without allowing the bad into our relationship avoiding what is everything that can do us any harm or generate anything that will give us a bad reputation.

Because if we don't know how to reject bad influences, we will surely be defeated.

It turns out that generally, bad influence presents itself as harmless and pleasant. At first, it conceals its true personality when the truth is it is bad or full of addictions. Whether small and large, it can negatively influence our behavior and even cause serious damage to everything and everyone around us, stealing, killing, and destroying our dreams.

Unfortunately, it is a harsh reality in our human society, do you agree?

So, what should we do to defend ourselves from such a dangerous situation?

We must be more vigilant and attentive because, as we know, that fun "friendship," an apparently pleasant company, can sometimes be the most dangerous one, the one that most impedes our development and the consequent success that we can achieve.

That person implicitly has a noxious temper, a negative "energy" caused by its bad thoughts, attitudes, which may still be hidden from us at a first impression.

But if we are vigilant, focused on the intentions, we will certainly find the truth.

Let us be attentive to examine those who cross our path, attempting to enter our relationship, with all wisdom, tranquility, cordiality, and naturalness, in the case that there is an absence of sincere intentions.

We should practice at the appropriate time the strength and the certainty of knowing how to say YES to everything good and just, and the powerful attitude of saying NO to everything bad and unjust. Suppose we sacrifice our natural tendency to be betrayed and deceived by appearances. Eventually, we start using our discernment to see through them.

By paying close attention to the factors surrounding the circumstances and sacrificing those usual distractions that routinely insist on getting involved, especially at the exact moment when we have to exercise valuable judgment and common sense, we will find perspicacity and be more invulnerable, succeeding in everything we really want to be.

Now, without losing focus, how about remembering our valued Heroes?

Is it possible to imagine how many anonymous Heroes exist in the World?

Bypassing with a more attentive look, we will see and be moved by the great sacrifices that Firefighters, Rescue Workers, Paramedics and Lifeguards, Police, Military, and all those who serve in the Armed Forces around the world do to defend everyone's life. And what about the War Veterans and all those who remain in front of the Battlefield to preserve the Free World, putting their own lives at risk day by day to protect us, even while we sleep!

How many times have doctors, nurses, and all other important medical professionals been at risk of dangerous contamination?

And how many people are working to help, in the face of a global and deadly pandemic caused by the Covid19 Virus?

It is also worth mentioning the sacrifice that all Heroes, known or anonymous, make when they have to leave their families and those they love most for a certain time to keep them safe?

It is admirable and inspiring!

It goes much further.

How about we stop for a moment and venture a little further, using the power of imagination, to consider the incredible experience lived by this select group of professionals. Let us try to imagine the feelings and emotions at a whole nother level of sacrifice so that others may prosper.

It is impressive, regardless of everything we have seen, how humanity has to fight for survival and, at the same time, seek to improve it!

Now, let us together try to achieve the intensity of everything that occurs within each of these fearless human beings' circumstances.

With this reflection, we can clearly see how practically countless are all those who sacrifice themselves day by day for innumerable reasons and different purposes.

Imagine "take a look and see" the exact moment when an Astronaut embarks from his place of comfort, from among those he loves most, from the coexistence of his great love, his new passion, or his family and friends.

What do they feel about saying goodbye to all their loved ones and leaving on the most fantastic and dangerous space trip, where they will put their limits, dreams, and lives at risk towards the infinite and unknown Universe?

There is nothing more unknown, surprising, and at the same time so dangerous than traveling to space.

We are totally dependent on our Planet, its Gravity, and Atmosphere. Its environment rich in oxygen allows us to breathe, abundant in the water that quenches our thirst and hydrates us, very fertile in foods that give us energy and nourishment. Forces so necessary to our organism, in addition to all the other resources that keep us alive, healthy, productive, and in constant development.

To perceive the grandeur in all that we are reflecting is wonderful, very interesting. It moves our emotions, inspires our imagination's most fantastic visions, isn't it?

And speaking of imagination, try to think and imagine the takeoff of a spaceship or a rocket on a trip to the Moon. Traveling towards the distant and infinite space to do maintenance and update Satellites or a Space Station, even fulfill secret missions.

On the night of December 20, 2019, the President of the United States of America, Mr. Donald J. Trump, created the USSF - US SPACE FORCE (Space Force of the United States of America).

A fact of enormous, unprecedented achievement that only further expands its strong Global leadership, setting the flag of the United States of America at the highest point ever reached by humanity and establishing its dominance in the immensity of the vast and grand infinite Space.

For this reason, the trend from now on is that more and more men and women are working in Space to defend the security of our Planet, of everyone and their nations, in the most varied functions of exploration and development.

All the efforts that the Free World Leaders, Astronauts, and all of their Aerospace Industry have made and will continue to do in the fulfillment of their mandates, duties, and responsibilities, in their respective careers. The incredibly dangerous and challenging missions are really unique. Their lives surpass all limits in search of success, to encourage all humanity to make great leaps of discovery, raising all levels of technological evolution. All to consolidate the conquest of the vastness of Space in the Fantastic and always surprising Universe. For the benefit and prosperity of all of us who live on this extraordinary Blue Planet that we call EARTH!

How many and how many acts of sacrifice are made every day in the world?

Every day our "Anonymous Heroes" fight in an endless battle.

The Armed Forces, Security, Special Forces, and Intelligence Agencies and Federal Bureaus are a good example of this.

What about the Secret Service Agents of the Free World who give their lives to defend and save their President's life?

How many of them have been injured and even killed on the job?

How many more fearless and courageous people who even put themselves in the line of fire to save other people's lives on instinct, in an attitude of extreme courage, love, and sacrifice?

Certainly, there are many and even millions that make up this large number, correct?

How many reacted instinctively, by unexpected reflex, during an assault, to save the life of an innocent person known or even an unknown person or their great love?

This takes me back to 1992 when I was engaged to Sonia, who is now my wife.

One beautiful summer night, after having dinner, we were talking and reviewing all the preparations for our wedding, and the "magic" moment when I surprised my bride with a gift. I can still feel the emotion of her contagious smile at that very moment, when she was surprised by a gift box and even more the thoughtfulness of my gift to her. She hugged me, looked into my eyes, thanked and kissed me for a long time, and then immediately opened the box "charmed with a golden Swiss watch tailored to her taste."

At that point, we were already celebrating our love and the fulfillment of the dream of building a family, a new life together, and all the emotion that precedes a wedding and the projection of our plans for the future.

After that "wonderful and magical moment," when our smiles were stamped on her face, announcing the great happiness we were living in, I went to take her home, as I did every night because we were practically neighbors. She lived 500 meters, more or less, from my house. We were walking hand in hand, and when we were about 200 meters to her house, a car sud-denly came to a sudden stop on the corner and sped towards us, and the driver stopped aggres-sively in front of us. Four other assailants got out and pointed their weapons at us. We couldn't resist, we gave them all of our belongings, as they demanded. However, in a sudden moment right before they were about to get in the car and flee, one of them pulled his weapon and tried to pull my soon to be bride, probably to kidnap her and take her away with them. It was at that time, as fast as "lightning descends from the sky," that split second, an attitude of courage took over me and impelled me to stop our assailant from getting closer to her. I blocked him with all my strength and faced everyone bluntly, with such authority and intervention from GOD. I yelled out with a loud voice saying: don't you dare put your hands on her!

The bandit immediately stepped back, and the others did the same thing. They got in the car and left quickly, and the worst did not happen, fortunately!

Reflecting on this, why did I have this attitude?

Why did Sônia stand firm?

Why was Sônia delivered from that kidnapping attempt?

Why were we saved?

First of all, we were marked by LOVE, COMPASSION, and the MERCY of GOD who saved our lives, according to His Will.

I will never forget the supernatural experience, where my bride and I were saved by GOD. He showed us what to do in the face of that terrible assault. And it was there, the place HE chose to teach me how to make the full sacrifice, risking his life for true love. HE, also gave us the courage, the strength, the Words and the attitude of his Power, so that together we would overcome that "darkness" that was trying to destroy our dreams.

A sacrifice for true love can move heaven in your favor and bring down the Power of GOD over you!

It can also be in your life, where all opposition will be removed. Everything that gets in your way hurts you and prevents you from growing and prospering will flee your presence if you focus your eyes on the light and walk on the correct path. Prioritize what really matters, "aiming at the right mark," aiming to achieve all objectives with strong work, dedication, firmness, and integrity.

Keep an eye on the details in your day-to-day, and if you notice that there is something inconvenient or wrong in your life, even though it's something you like a lot, it gives you pleasure and some satisfaction to your body, soul, and spirit. Act quickly, correct this mistake, and remove it from your life. Take a firm attitude of sacrificing that "pleasure" for truth and love. Totally conscious and without looking back, you will certainly prevail because there is a lot of honor inside the act of courage of sacrificing for a greater good. It starts within yourself to achieve better quality in your life. Remember that the human body is incredible, but at the same time, it suffers and dies. In contrast, our soul and spirit are eternal! After acting in this way, you will feel motivated to help others. You will help the neediest, such as taking an exceptional action to save a helpless child's life and every innocent person you can, according to your strengths.

Life here on earth passes very quickly, and we fly!

Accomplish and do everything excellently with all the goodwill.

Be kind.

Preserve the peace.

Smile, transmit light and life.

Have faith that tomorrow can be better.

If you walk with a conscience, wisdom will reach you and be your best friend!

Remember that before the instinct for courage and the attitude of sacrifice, unconditional love for preserving life must be present.

Believe that far beyond our vision is the origin of life; it is also born making sacrifices!

Chapter 9

ACQUIRING WISDOM

After all, what is WISDOM?

Certainly, everyone has their opinion about this provocative theme that affects our imagination so much, right?

However, I tell you in a very peculiar and personal way that, in my view, WISDOM is to acquire knowledge and use it intelligently for the greater good.

Where does WISDOM come from?

WISDOM comes from GOD!

With WISDOM, he created all things visible and invisible, including us and the dimension where the world we live in, in this challenging now, called our time!

WISDOM is rare and precious!

In it lies the genesis, the strength and the power, the majesty and the beauty, the grandeur, and the balance of everything!

Close your eyes and try to remember everything perfectly!

Push your memory to its limit of your imagination!

See the greatness, the multiplicity, and witness the infinity that is in all creation!

The fantastic Universe that we know so little about is great and incomparable. We see it from this magnificent Earth, our home, where we were born and developed. We can observe all this fascinating and powerful nature surrounding us, that shelters and sustains our life.

Furthermore, looking from here to the distant and infinite blue sky, and seeing through the images captured by the lenses of telescopes, satellites, probes, incredible spaceships, and their cameras, we marvel at everything that is within reach of our vision.

Each day, we seek more wisdom to explore its immensity and discover what is beyond our vision in the vastness of this unpredictable and uncontrollable Universe.

Such power and incredible beauty make this Universe so fantastic and extraordinary that its magnitude is difficult to comprehend!

As we pay attention and do a quick reflection, we are fascinated to realize that WISDOM is an endless and limitless power, capable of going much further to create, produce, and prosper all other worlds and everything in them.

How magnificent to be able to contemplate this wonder and still be able to imagine what must be further beyond!

WISDOM gives us discernment, reason, judgment, common sense, and the attitude of knowing how to choose the best of doing what is right, even when we are under strong pressure.

It's impressive!

When we reflect on this interesting topic, we are incredibly motivated, don't you agree?

It gives us the conditions and the power, and it adds every day in each of us the inspiration, the creative capacity, the strength, and the attributes needed to create.

Think and try to remember how many inventions have already been developed by the human species?

How many achievements?

How many great discoveries?

How many technologies?

From the age of fire to the present, how many were WISDOM's achievements for the prosperity of humanity?

What about intelligence, ingenuity, and human efficiency that created controlling water methods and developed prosperous Food Production?

What technology has modernized our way of dressing and revolutionized the clothing industry and commerce that continues expanding?

In our houses' construction process generated and still generates today the different cities' different compositions that shape our World?

And what about the creation of our vibrant and diverse Industries?

It is the Industries that form the solid foundation of a rich, strong, and vibrant national economy.

Its essential sectors continue to impact us, do you agree?

And yet, they remain in constant evolution.

Observe the characteristics of our main Industries:

The food industry that was harvested from farms, and the precious achievement of producing drinking water, without which there would be no healthy life. Consequently, we would not have consolidated the quality of products derived from our Agriculture, Livestock, Fisheries, and other industrial productions.

Steel companies formed the pillar of our economy's solidity, feeding all industrial segments and building indelibly. It is the victorious mark of the development trajectory of humanity, which comes from the precious Gold, Silver, Bronze, the strength of Steel, the resistance of Copper, the longevity of Aluminum, the resilience of Titanium, to the power of invulnerability of the incredible Niobium. Going through every fantastic periodic table of the minerals already discovered, until the incredible journey in search of those that we will still discover.

Civil Construction and its entire industry, especially the revolution of Concrete, which together with Steel, Glass, Petroleum, and its derivatives, adding many others with coatings, brought our existence magnificent cities and their gigantic "skyscrapers."

Pharmaceuticals provide all kinds of drugs that prevent, treat, and cure diseases.

Medical Products that protect us help us make a huge difference in favor of developing new technologies capable of improving, surprising, and even saving lives.

From Oil, Gas, and its derivatives, to Nuclear, which together will certainly be replaced by other sources of clean and renewable energy. Giving everyone much power in each generation and incomparable security.

From Bioenergy, from the essential Ethanol, from other Biofuels to its more distant derivatives, a conscious use can collaborate with the healthier maintenance of our environment. We help clean up our air, water, and forests, strengthen our quality of life, and even collaborate to save our planet.

Joining forces with those that produce and distribute Clean Energy, from the Solar, through the Wind, to the impressive Tidal Wave ; Naval, Automobile, Aeronautics, and even Aerospace.

Appliances and Electronics, Equipment, Tools, Accessories, and all sorts of integral products so necessary for this "gear" to move and make our economy develop, grow, and prosper.

From Telecommunications, from Radio, Telex, to the impressive Telephone, from surprising Television to the "magical" Internet.

The Arts, Music, Theater, Cinema and showbiz, Television and Plastic Arts, which join all the others in this exciting sector, make our great cultural diversity and vibrate.

Computer science with the invention and compacting of the extraordinary computer that today fits incredibly in the palm of our hands.

And with its great capacity and almost infinite use, which has revolutionized all other Industries and practically everything in our society?

There is still much more yet waiting for us to achieve and discover, right?

Look:

How many other important technological leaps have the Human Society made in its development trajectory?

What of the incredible skill that created all sorts of engineering for everything and much more is yet to be created?

How many times do we believe that we had reached the summit of all scientific knowledge of a given technology?

And when we least expect it, we take a new leap in technological evolution, such as:

What happened in telecommunications' trajectory, from the invention of the telephone to the Wi-Fi internet and all wireless communication technology.

What an evolution !!!

It is exciting to witness the unimaginable, unlikely to us, happened and surprised all of us, isn't it?

And the most interesting and curious thing is that in the case of the phone, many believed that it would take much longer for it to develop, to modernize because the technological capacity of the phone was limited for a long time and suddenly took a giant technological leap surprising everyone, wasn't it?

And it is still in constant development and evolution, right?

There are so many discoveries and achievements that WISDOM has already provided humanity that we would have to write a great book entirely dedicated to this theme so that all these achievements could fit in its pages so that we could count them all!

We would still have to continue writing other great books on this same topic, to register the knowledge given us each day.

How many new technologies are ready and waiting for us to be discovered?

How many old and new Worlds await us?

How many new forms of life are yet to be discovered on our Planet, within the dimension of the unknown infinite, in other Universes, and much more beyond? Have you really tried to imagine how many new lives are born every second?

Traveling through time...the invention of the wheel, through the creation and evolution of the automobile, the invention of the airplane, of ships, aircraft carriers, and nuclear submarines, supersonic jets, to the incredible success of rockets, and the fantastic spaceships, which they defy gravity by traveling at ever faster speeds, breaking boundaries and going further and further exploring the vastness of this infinite Universe.

Think of the great inventions rich in Wisdom, which created the different sectors of our economy and tried to imagine this inventive process's entire trajectory. The great technological ingenuity:

- Building our Industries.

- Boosting Commerce.

- Expanding our Service network to become even bigger and much better than we could have predicted or imagined.

It is always impressive and curiously incredible to know that all these achievements were brought to light by our dimension through the knowledge revealed to us by WISDOM's strong presence revolutionizing everything that was before! And also to think that all that exists is the result of just a spark, the spark of WISDOM!!!

Certainly, such knowledge is wonderful and motivates us to further search for new achievements.

All of this brings to mind the request that King Solomon made to GOD when he had the opportunity to ask him what he wanted, and He only asked for WISDOM!

As written in the Old Testament of our Bible, in 1 Kings 3: 3-14.

Let's highlight the words described in 1 Kings 3: 5, and 9.

"At Gibeon the Lord appeared to Solomon during the night in a dream, and God said, Ask for whatever you want me to give you."

"So give your servant a discerning heart to govern your people and to distinguish between right and wrong. For who is able to govern this great people of yours?"

As we witness the immense power of all the teachings contained in words of eternal wisdom, we are awakened, revived, and encouraged to win. Because, when we cry out to God for wisdom, such truth has the power to awaken the best within each one of us.

Chapter 10

CHALLENGING AND ELIMINATING THE PROBLEM

From an early age, we were accustomed to use the word "problem" to identify everything difficult, and practically impossible to be solved and everything that afflicts us and takes away peace.

In an involuntary and almost imperceptible way, we reproduce the error of those who formed such a word in our language. And it was exactly there that we created a "monster," opponent, the enemy, similar to a "demon" that is called "problem."

That's the name of the one who opposes us, and it is also what generates tribulations in our dimension.

It is the one that always tries to intimidate us, to prevent our victory, our triumph, our achievements, and to surpass our goals so that we can never achieve our improvement and consequently not achieve success.

Even when we accept that name to identify the meaning of almost all ills, the diseases in our health, the damage we suffer in different areas, the obstacles and barriers that come our way, the difficult issues, which cause us harm, and even the storms and the unexplainable are those things that seem negative to us.

Did you know that in doing so, unconsciously, of course, we are taking away our own ability to produce and generate the response vital for creating solutions to overcome the difficult circumstances of life?

On the other hand, we gave this strength that we took from ourselves, without realizing it, surrendering it to the "monster" called problem.

We begin to view things from the bottom up and view ourselves as tiny, and it is a giant.

In other words:

The problem became "owner of the circumstances," causing anxiety, fear, even the word "headache" associated with it, and in an "avalanche" of "somatizations" and symptomatic psychological confusion, which causes emotional damage, nervousness, and irritability.

Soon it turns into pains and physical disorders, which radiate throughout the body, starting with the head, stomach, covering the bones, muscles, and important organs, making our whole body suffer. Remember that all this damage is caused to us because we unintentionally created a "monster," we labeled a problem. We started to give its name to everything that makes life difficult.

Incredible as it may seem, even the unexpected of everyday life, we give this label. We do not stop there. We also learn to label all the bad climate of this time that presents itself before us. Sometimes by a distraction, sometimes by an involuntary questioning ourselves, things caused by other people, for events, or for other situations that are beyond our control. What I mean is that instead of giving a name of the power that would bring our existence to the strength of the solution, we created a "terrible" word and strengthened this old and "evil" adversary of our lives, called problem.

After reflecting on such things, it is always good to remember to dominate the surprising and important subjects, similar to our analysis. It is essential to seek the answers in the same place where we found them a long time ago, when we began this study, to overcome the negativity contained in that word.

In a special source, known as the Greatest Book of All Time, which is also an insurmountable record of eternal wisdom, and the only Book capable of clarifying any doubts, including those on this difficult subject, and the name of this powerful Book is The HOLY BIBLE.

The book of all books, never was and never will be another beautiful book in which we can stand firm, widespread or propagated, respected, record holder, and opinion-maker than our BIBLE!

It's what motivates us to pause here to go on the record saying that this has been tested through time and remains today, the greatest literary legacy in GOD's history for us.

He is continually teaching us to live with quality and newness of life, to preserve the salvation that came to us through the infinite grace of God Himself, when He revealed himself to all, through the immense love and incomparable sacrifice, that His Son Only-begotten, JESUS CHRIST consumed in our favor. When he gave humanity the incredible opportunity to be reconciled with God, the Father, and Creator of everything.

Now, going back to where we left off; we also discovered that the word *problem* does not exist in the Bible. It does not exist in the book of life. Therefore, we can safely say that this word is not part of GOD's language, nor of the language that He created for all of us to communicate efficiently.

Because as we may already know, words have the power of the meanings we give them, don't they? We believe that they have the power to help us build our success, if we use the right words and use them in the right way. Using them with wisdom and intelligence, at the right time, respecting each one's meaning and applying them in the most appropriate circumstances.

However, we also believe that words have the power to help us destroy our success if we do the opposite. When we use the wrong words in the wrong way, without wisdom or intelligence, disrespecting the meaning of each of them and applying them in the most inappropriate circumstances.

Proceeding to our "target," without losing focus, we reasoned and managed to understand that the word problem should not even exist in our vocabulary.

It is important to remember that the word *problem* does not exist in GOD's vocabulary. Earlier I said that it shouldn't exist in the human vocabulary. Because if we really want to win, we must be the "mirror" of GOD's teachings reflected through our behaviors, built and defined by thoughts, intentions, temperaments, and attitudes.

Remember that the way we act most of the time is dependent on and comes from the way we construct our thoughts. Therefore, what we think can determine how we act and react under the circumstances. Consequently, we will have the ability to shape the construction of our character, the behavior of all of us, and influence the limit of our achievements and even determine who we will become in our day.

Therefore, this and other negative words that undermine and steal our strength must not affect us.

We are going to break the code and destroy all the "evil" meaning of negative words, using as our "weapon" the power that exists in the meanings of positive words. Even the dictionaries' anonymous words oppose negative words, helping us to exclude them from our vocabulary by replacing them with words that correctly characterize the difficult circumstances of life, but motivate us to overcome them!

With total FAITH!

Courage!

Determination!

Energy!

How about we remove the word *problem* that takes away the strength of self-esteem that is fundamental and gives us the courage, in addition to everything else we need, to solve successfully, day by day, the most varied and even complicated questions, and putting in its place the word that challenges all our adversities.

Also, depending on the circumstances, we include in this vocabulary, other words that are synonymous with difficult and challenging situations, such as:

Difficulty, obstacle, unforeseen, setback, complication, misfortune, tribulation, inconvenience, setback, discomfort, annoyance, impediment, uncertainty, obstacle, resistance, and opposition. Because in doing so, we take charge!

We put ourselves in a privileged and fully motivated position to overcome any tribulations. We will then begin to realize the incredible change that cancels what is negative and enhances what is positive.

However, it is a gradual process that will efficiently build this new super positive reaction force. It doesn't happen suddenly as if by magic.

On the contrary, we will have to dedicate ourselves and do our part, but when we take this attitude of substituting the word *problem* for the word *challenge*, we take control. When we take control, we will have much more control and suffer much less opposition to overcome any adversity.

From the small obstacles to the great challenges, whatever it is, we will be motivated, compelled to overcome it, because, in this way, we will be able to annihilate and all the difficulties that arise before us "transforming it into dust blown by the wind."

Another advantage that we will acquire is that we no longer suffer in anticipation, where we will have the chance to eliminate the "old and stubborn" words associated with the word "evil," and incorrectly call it a *problem*, which causes damage to everyone who uses it.

If we close our eyes and remember when we use the word problem to identify a particular difficulty we were experiencing, we can certainly see that at that time, we felt diminutive in front of it.

However, if we do exactly the opposite, we will undoubtedly be motivated with all courage through the exercise of identifying our difficulties and calling them *challenges*. Certainly, we can feel much more consequential than all of them.

Do you understand the difference and power of this simple and intelligent attitude?

Here is an extraordinary reason, and it is worth repeating:

From now on, honestly try, in times of adversity, to develop this method that we are teaching here, using your mental strength, and then put it into practice, saying: Today, I have a challenge.

I believe that you will realize that you will be much more encouraged and able to face and fight to overcome these difficult moments in life because they will have labeled and applied the word *challenge* correctly.

In doing so you will be confronting the challenge instead of being confronted by it, and in doing so, you will also cease to be the object of the action, being subject to your reaction. Did you notice how everything gets simpler? After all, this book's idea is also to teach us to simplify the day-to-day of our lives. Beginning with our thoughts and going as far as our attitudes.

It will never be too much to repeat the importance to remember to cultivate what is good!

To practice the good!

To live on Earth with goodwill and to preserve peace!

To be happy and not look back!

To look forward!

Look up to the blue sky above, where the help and answer you are looking for will always come from!

Just as it is when you look to faith within you. Do not be afraid because GOD is with you.

It is surprising how, in the Christian Bible, the word or words similar to "do not fear" are written 365 times. There is a message of courage in the Bible that gives us the power to eliminate fear and use it every day of the year. Fear not!!!

GOD really takes this issue very seriously, and it is He who enables us to overcome all of our fears with the simplicity in his Words; He teaches us to take possession of the meaning of each word, nullifying any opposing negative words of defeat that still insists on being part of our vocabulary.

Never forget that we were born to win!

Never let anything or anyone stop you.

After all, all who believe and live the teachings of JESUS are more than conquerors and children of GOD, knowing that our Kingdom is the Eternal Kingdom!

Chapter 11

* FACING TRIBULATIONS
WITH FAITH
AND COURAGE *

Tribulation.

Tribulation is an ancient historical word, well known and widespread in the human language.

A Biblical term present in both the Old and New Testaments.

The most impressive thing is that this word and its synonyms are present in all the main books of religions in the world.

It challenges humanity so much, from antiquity to the present day.

It crosses generations and confronts our limit. For some, it will be like this until the end, and a new beginning for others.

However, we have to be of good cheer because we mature and are perfected when we face tribulations.

How many challenging situations have we all experienced today?

How many times have we been weak and, in an almost "supernatural" way, get up and proceed to our target?

How many times have we faced "no" and how many other times with "yes?"

If we pay close attention, we will discover that the "no" we received was given to us by life and never by tribulation. Because life is so wonderful that it only protects and preserves us and strives to keep us safe and well. And to prove this fact, it is enough to observe the creation of life and all that it gives us. So, we must not forget that it did not come from tribulation when we received no, but from life.

the consciousness that dwells deep within our being, that belongs to life, turns on a light of understanding warning us. That what we want, all though looks good to our eyes, in fact, is a poison, which would certainly do us much harm. We thus understand that life is also one that saves us from danger and tribulation. LIFE is a treasure!

We can never compare LIFE with what afflicts us.

Did you realize that the "key" to this understanding is knowing how to discern such things and make the perfect separation between tribulation and LIFE?

We can no longer commit this primary error and involuntary act, which is to attribute everything bad to life as if the will of life created evil.

When we observe calmly, we can clearly see that life gives life, the light, and there is no darkness in it. Therefore, if we want to overcome the tribulation, we must know how to separate the tribulation and what is actually LIFE.

Did you see how everything becomes lighter and more and more simple if we think and act like that?

Proceeding without fear and with much more understanding along this path, consider the following:

How many tribulations have you faced in your life?

None,

One,

Two,

or three?

How many?

Each of us has our own particular experiences, right?

History is being built on this journey and the trials of life!

How much tribulation has humanity suffered?

When reflecting on this theme, we are faced with an almost unanimous result and opinions when we realize that we are the targets of tribulations at some point in life.

I sincerely tell you that I do not know any human being who has lived without suffering or without going through or facing tribulation.

It is important to mention that our ancestors formed through time and historical records, an inexhaustible source of information and research of all their experiences lived along their trajectories. Consequently a strong legacy of experience, as we have also had the pleasure to register here to illustrate and reflect carefully.

And, as well as enjoying citing them, and still have the habit of even paying them a tribute, recognizing the great historical and cultural heritage that each of them left behind for each of us. How about we venture out one little more and delve into this reflection?

Now, speaking of our ancestors and drawing attention to them again, we could not fail to emphasize that we have learned great lessons by remembering them. We have a chance to not make the same mistakes that they did, as well as, of mirroring ourselves in all the good they did, to commit the same things they did, and more, we can still perfect all those things that reflect all the good things they did, and what they achieved, to apply in our lives.

I tell you that in our present day, we should not be frightened by tribulation. Quite the contrary, we have already learned that in the midst of this life's adversities, we must stimulate and encourage ourselves, motivate ourselves to face, go through, overcome, and defeat each one that is placed before us and before those for whom we have the "call" to help, defend, preserve, and protect!

We have a choice!

We always did and always will have a choice.

Our life always gives us choices at some point. And when we look at this from the outside, looking into the circumstances, we can see those opportunities!

Imagine a beautiful garden in the shape of a large labyrinth, very common in landscaping worldwide, in the Americas, Europe, Asia, and Africa, emphasizing its western spread by the strong presence of European colonization since antiquity.

And when we look at the circumstances that caused the tribulation, as if we had an eagle's view, we can unveil this labyrinth.

That's when we can identify it very clearly. By clearly identifying the causes of the tribulation, we have the chance to study the weaknesses that each one has so that we can prepare a perfect combat tactic, to get it right on target, where the tribulation is weakest, where it is exposed. There is where we have to hit harder and harder until we overthrow it. All of this is possible if we practice discipline. When we look without fear at the tribulation. And the best part is that we will overcome it; it will also help us teach others how to overcome. Because everything we learn is to teach and transfer and propagate from generation to generation.

Because it is enough for this knowledge to arrive to encourage everyone who is being afflicted. So that all those afflicted may be immediately stimulated, strongly encouraged, and motivated to face the roadblocks, overcome and conquer each of their tribulations to achieve success. So that they may immediately get out of a dark situation brought on by the tribulation and come to light and contemplate the peace that is in our victory.

Facing and overcoming tribulations is imperative and undoubtedly, the greatest of our challenges because every tribulation is dangerous and brings all kinds of evil and darkness.

In the beginning, it generates a little anxiety, a silent restlessness that grows, making soft sounds until it becomes a noise that causes oppression, which gradually suffocates us until it becomes depression, waiting to attack our body after it is weakened.

And from the plausibility of depression in our soul, it can produce a deep sadness damaging our emotions, confusing our thoughts, trying all the time to annul our self-esteem. With it the bad intention of producing discouragement, weakening of spirit, low self-esteem, and intimidation, causing the inability even to be able to reason lucidly, to find the solutions we so badly need to win.

And it does not stop there. Discouragement is a disease that tries to cause the numbness of our spirit and our soul's.

Unfortunately, many of our brothers fall victims to the tribulation that caused them to fall. As we just analyzed, with an uncontrollable desire to give up everything, they could not find a solution. Believing then that there no longer was hope.

See then that if we really want to win, we need to be proactive. For that, it is necessary to pay close attention to the events and signals emitted by society, which are amplified and reported through all the media sources, which besides being many and different from each other, it can also change at any moment, depending on each circumstance.

We continuously ought to anticipate adversity, observing everything that is most relevant, remaining focused on those signs that precede any tribulation in our path.

However, I warn you to watch and make good use of the strategies frequently. Practice the tactics in our study and, with wisdom and courage, fight all the evil process of tribulation that we describe in detail here. Discern every step of your behavior to expose your weaknesses to be defeated by you every time it tries to take over you.

By observing all this attack, that tribulation insists on making on us human beings, especially if we are not vigilant by protecting our balance at all times, to quickly identify and defeat the anxiety that always comes within it, aiming to gain more self-control over every situation, in addition to preserving it and using it as a powerful weapon to win.

Remember always to exercise the incredible strength of self-esteem, breaking the storm, seeing the light and sun that represent our victory, our success, our bliss, leaping in faith, without looking down for fear of falling, without doubting, because GOD is and will support you because his purpose is good!

Fighting with courage!

Living with courage!

Making the sacrifice!

For the children of GOD, in this dimension, in this world, without sacrifice, there is no victory! Receive the wisdom that comes from above, the Throne of GOD!

It gives you the power to challenge, over-come adversity, cancel, and banish the word *problem* from your vocabulary and history. To face, overcome, and go through the tribu-lation! My brothers and sisters, as the apostle Paul received the inspiration of GOD, through JESUS CHRIST, I tell you that every tribulation produces in us perseverance.

Perseverance, experience, and hope in an extraordinary way gives us the power of faith, and with the power of faith, hope overcomes fear!

Do not be discouraged because we all have a purpose; to achieve the purpose of our lives, we must fight with courage and strength.

It takes a lot of discipline to overcome each of the difficult circumstances that come against us.

Nothing can stop us because we are encouraged to build a very precious Family!

Here at this moment, I see a huge opportunity before us, which is to rewrite our history, transform our world, our society, and our community, starting with our home, as well as our relationships everywhere in the environment that we live in, into something tremendously happy.

I believe in happiness!

In a child's smile!

How much innocence is there in a child's smile?

How much love?

Just imagining it is fantastic and exciting!

And the most extraordinary thing about this is that innocence is powerful too, and we learn that innocence is the absence of guilt.

Notice that in the Bible, the book of Psalms in the Old Testament, King David, in chapter 26, verse 6, while crying out to the LORD GOD, exclaimed saying:

"I wash my hands in innocence, and go about your altar, LORD,"

Then see how innocence is special, of great importance, and extraordinary restorative force that to purify himself and get closer to the ETERNAL GOD, King David declares before the Lord that he would wash his hands in innocence, how precious and powerful what is revealed here. His innocence is full of love. That is the greatest of the powers we know!

So, remember to smile every day and know that you can overcome all tribulations.

We cannot fail to pay attention if we must tactically, strategically face that tribulation in the form of a direct confrontation. There are circumstances where the best way to overcome a tribulation is to stay away from it; yes, move away and go very far from it, because when we do that, it loses strength, it dries up and dies; totally dehydrated, "as a person who needs water and does not receive, and therefore dehydrates and dies," so is the tribulation, it suffers dies when you understand that you should not, in that situation, use confrontation as the best weapon to beat it.

On many occasions, it is better to confuse it by walking away from it because in doing so, the tribulation will be blind and will not have "eyes for you."

As we talked about earlier, you have a choice; we all have choices, and by making the right choice, we step out of sight of the "enemy" who is represented by the tribulation, the enemy of life.

And when we do that, it won't be able to reach us anymore.

So, remember!

Calmly evaluate the situation before taking action, knowing the cause of each tribulation that stands before you. Wisely assess whether a confrontation is necessary or its better to walk away and deviate from it.

Walk away happily in peace, on your beautiful path because you have a choice!

So, make the right choice!

See how much GOD is teaching us in our walk and bringing these things to our memory.

Let's not forget that our thoughts are in full use; through the imaginations that arise while reading, the power of thought is incredible and extraordinary.

Always have positive thoughts!

How many answers, from the simplest to the most difficult, can GOD be giving us right now?

See how much He is inspiring us to seek more and more of His wisdom to learn how to overcome tribulation?

We strategically highlight places in each chapter, at every opportunity, and at every appropriate moment, to be unveiled by you in this book.

A mark that comes from a truth that only brings us peace.

It is a mark showing words of wisdom in GOD's teachings, through his greatest revelation: JESUS CHRIST.

And speaking of JESUS, it is worth remembering something fascinating that He told us and has everything to do with the theme of this chapter when He told us and recorded by the Apostle John, in chapter 16, verse 33, of the Gospels of the New Testament of our Christian Bible:

"I have told you these things, so that in me you may have peace. In this world you will have trouble. But take heart! I have overcome the world."

So, because He won and He won it all, and even when He conquered death and reconciled us to GOD, we will also win. Through His New Covenant of love, freedom, and grace, for everyone who really wants to have a relationship with Him, for those who really want to walk with GOD.

It is exciting because it is an eternal alliance of freedom and everything good that comes from GOD, to bless his children, provides us with understanding and the preservation of true freedom! Freedom is a tremendous asset, and it is only when we learn to face, go through, and overcome tribulations that we truly earn our freedom. And it is the freedom that GOD has given us that brings us perfect peace, prosperity, and fullness of love.

Build on those bases!

Live these principles with a strong purpose in your life!

Use all the powerful meaning contained in each word of wisdom, which translates into "heavy weaponry," capable of annihilating all opposition to your success.

Be especially aware of the signs around you all the time. They are revealing GOD's plans and dreams for your life.

Pay attention to details! Stay focused on your goal!

Devote yourself to planning and create a strategy capable of overcoming obstacles!

Make a tactical plan and put it into practice to overcome adversity's limits and reach your goals!

Focus and build with your powerful mind, using all your faith. The discipline of intelligence combined with a strong commitment to conquer attracts to you everything you need most.

Bring your success from dream to reality!

Never be intimidated by the difficulties that come with tribulations.

Because GOD is Much Greater and is above all! Remember that HE IS your Creator! Let the "fire" of the Power of Faith live in your memory! Always remember who you are!

Counter the tribulation with all the strength of self-esteem that exists within you! Because you can beat each one! Fight and never let your guard down! Stay in the "Watchtower." Always be encouraged to overcome all tribulations, because with God, all things are possible for us!

With GOD "we tear down impassable walls!" And with this inspiration, we take the opportunity to bring to mind a biblical, historical, and extraordinary truth. It is a word from GOD that also translates from our ancestors' experience, from Genesis to Revelation that strengthens our Faith. As it is written in our Christian Bible, by the Apostle Paul, inspired by JESUS CHRIST, in a letter to the Romans, in chapter 8, verse 28:

"And we know that in all things God works for the good of those who love him, who have been called according to his purpose."

It is fantastic to understand this truth, which brings us the happiness of knowing how the trajectory of our ancestors was recorded throughout human history, proving that all things together cooperate for the good of those who love GOD!

Chapter 12

*WITH THE STRENGTH
OF PERSEVERANCE*

We learned that extraordinarily all tribulation produces in us the STRENGTH OF
PERSEVERANCE.

After all, what is PERSEVERANCE?

Certainly, each of us has an answer and an
explanation.

The various dictionaries cataloged in millions
of libraries worldwide also have the meaning

and all also the well-known synonyms of the word PERSEVERANCE.

There are several opinions and different definitions about this and any word that forms human language.

Living the challenges brought about by various tribulations throughout my life, I learned that PERSEVERANCE is, above all, an attitude of faith; to believe without even doubting what you want.

In reality, it is never giving up working and continuing until you reach all the good things that you dreamed and planned to achieve success!

It is the STRENGTH that keeps self-esteem up there and very well protected within each one of us!

Knowing that circumstances do not define us or determine who we are and what kingdom we belong to.

Because as we have already learned, what actually defines us determines who we are, and what kingdom we belong to is the way we react under the circumstances!

Remembering that if we are not well today, we will soon be, because we believe, persevere, move on without looking back.

We always persist and never give up fighting for our dreams!

PERSEVERANCE <u>is keeping the flame </u>of HOPE burning!

It is the discipline of staying on target. Persisting because we know exactly the good purpose of our lives, in each of the different phases!

So, therefore, I also learned that PERSEVERANCE is to believe without doubting that the preservation of HOPE alive within us, guiding our thoughts, attitudes, and reactions, is what leads us to the better days that announce our triumph!

If we really want to win, we have to keep a firm and vigilant mind, to strengthen our behavior of never going back and never giving up!

Another significant point is always to clearly identify what motivates us to persevere.

It is necessary to make sure that what we are looking for is good, perfect, and pleasing to GOD, us, those we love, and our neighbor.

In fact, we persevere to make our lives a good declaration of success and a source of inspiration for many and the help for those who need so much help.

We persevere so that when they look at us, they do not see us but rather see the powerful presence of GOD, full of love, compassion, and mercy.

Yes, we persevere because in us dwells a spark of the Power of GOD, who gives us an excellent spirit, activated by His Holy Spirit who lives within us.

How many times have we faced circumstances of tremendous adversity, in which our PERSEVERANCE has made us overcome, achieve our goals, and achieve that difficult victory?

How many times did you have to persevere in the face of the tribulations of this time?

The fact is that we all know that in this world we live in, there are many difficulties and even countless pitfalls, temptations, and obstacles that appear before us to discourage us, intimidate us, make us stop, and prevent us from achieving our dreams, our goals, and purposes of life.

But, instead of being sad, we should rejoice, because in truth, as we have already seen, the tribulation produces PERSEVERANCE in us.

It is a light that inspires our mind, broadens our vision, surrounds us, and radiates throughout our being, and this is how we are truly strengthened, empowered, and motivated to win.

This opportunity also gives us something extraordinary, that is PATIENCE!

In this way, we discover that PERSEVERANCE creates in us PATIENCE!

Perseverance is for those who respect time.

Because there is a "God's time" in our lives, for the revelation of all things, to know that each of them only happens at the right time:

There is a time to plant!

Another time to cultivate!

And happy harvest time!

We believe that there is a specific time under our infinite blue sky, for the materialization of all things!

And this is one of many other stories that we will have the opportunity to share with you all in GOD's timing.

Here and now, in this very moment as we are sharing these wonderful teachings that come from GOD, concerning PERSEVERANCE, we insist on repeating several times to establish that it's what gives us the strength to overcome difficult moments, in those most vulnerable moments in this huge "battlefield" that is called the world.

Persevere!

Don't give up!

Because after each "wall" you cross, you will surely find your VICTORY! Live with PERSEVERANCE and face the challenges with the PATIENCE of WISDOM, which gives birth to BALANCE.

Keep the FOCUS on your target and what you want to achieve. Draw a STRATEGY of short, medium, or long term, according to each objective you want to achieve. Put SMART TACTICS into action and never forget to be humble at heart.

To be a motivating force in other lives, at all times, even when you are facing adversity and tribulation. Know how to separate yourself from them, looking from above and from the outside to keep the POWER of SELF-ESTIMATE vibrating in your life.

Always keep your mind and your five senses aligned with your soul and united with your spirit. All of them well adjusted, living in total harmony with the spark of the Holy Spirit of God, who dwells within us, inspiring and instructing us with His WISDOM, to do what is just, to promote a greater good, as our greatest purpose in life, and true prosperity.

This level of efficiency can only be achieved by persevering!

Do you see the importance of PERSEVERANCE?

Remembering that PERSEVERANCE is a mighty force! After all, we are dealing with POWER in this book; POWER to win!

So, it is worth mentioning that each chapter of this book contains a POWER formula for us to win!

Thrive!

We simplify and value life!

And PERSEVERANCE is one of the greatest gifts that GOD gives us, in the goal that we build SELF-ESTEEM:

Unbreakable!

Indestructible!

Able to resist all envy, slander, defamation, sabotage, all forms of evil against our lives.

Because PERSEVERANCE is contained in all the POWERS discussed here in this book since the first chapter.

So pay close attention, guard your thoughts, and cultivate PERSEVERANCE!

Make it develop and grow more and more in your life!

Build reasoning that maintains a constant, effective behavior and has SELF DOMAIN!

Always acting with firmness and integrity!

Living like this, you will experience the incomparable and extraordinary supernatural POWER of GOD in your life!

And you will certainly be surprised and even impacted by what you will be able to accomplish!

PERSEVERANCE is a sword that pierces every "enemy" who dares to stand as an obstacle to try to intimidate you and make you stop!

Chapter 13

*WITH THE FRUIT
OF EXPERIENCE*

EXPERIENCE!

EXPERIENCE, without a doubt, starts its presence in our lives even before we were born in this world. It grows with us and remains at our side as a great motivator for our improvement!

We believe that some questions remain intriguing, and that is why it is worth reflecting on them, to improve our understanding of this important word that is used to select, classify and even make valuable judgments, clarifying the efficiency of each of us, in the most varied situations. From the genesis of creation and production of all forms of life, accompanying us along this fantastic journey until we consolidate our footprints in the extraordinary "sands of time."

We invite you to think about this provocative topic and find your own answers to the following questions, in addition to many others that you feel motivated to ask:

☐ After all, what can we say about EXPERIENCE?

☐ What is it?

☐ How is it born in us?

☐ Where does it come from?

☐ Why is it so valuable, since the beginning of time and until present day?

☐ What is the best way to obtain it?

☐ Why are we so driven by having it and even dominating it?

☐ Why are we challenged to continually use its infinite forms, to succeed in life?

We also understand that PERSEVERANCE continuously produces and builds EXPERIENCE in us!

And what is EXPERIENCE, if not the source of the cause of our IMPROVEMENT?

Living each footprint that built the history of our lives!

If we pay close attention and do our part with dedication and courage, the immense POWER OF PERSEVERANCE will emerge in us, which will produce in each one fantastic and extraordinary EXPERIENCE.

All of this improvement creates a tremendous strength that keeps us steadfast and moving forward towards the purpose of our lives.

EXPERIENCE is strong enough to clarify the knowledge, yes, the solutions, which are brought into existence, with the ability to resolve each issue, however complicated it may be because it is full of WISDOM!

It reflects and consolidates all the knowledge and gifts we have acquired throughout this incredible, fantastic, and extraordinary journey!

And with each step, we have the chance to become wiser, to the same extent that we are perfected.

The most impressive thing is that even in the midst of difficulties brought to us by tribulations, we are presented with the POWER of PERSEVERANCE, producing the EXPERIENCE that perfects us with WISDOM.

Remembering that to be perfected in this way, we cannot be distracted by the illusions that always appear along the way.

On the contrary, it is imperative to maintain balance, focus, and have a strong purpose, allied to the humility of looking for signs of virtues, until we can clearly identify them. Taking advantage of the various growth opportunities that are contained in the most varied situations and also in each of the adversities that we go through during our surprising trajectory.

We have to consider that nowadays, with so many technologies, there is an even greater risk of being distracted, moving away from the main objective. So we will begin to pay much more attention to things that matter less, instead of dedicating ourselves to what is really important; the development of the GREAT VIRTUES and the consequent production of EXPERIENCE that form and strengthen in each of us, an EXCELLENT CHARACTER.

With this understanding that opens our vision, it is worth remembering again to look within us, where PERSEVERANCE resides, and up to where our SALVATION comes from!

These are very strong and even "supernatural" teachings, for many, because they come from the inspiration and infinite grace of GOD, recorded in the WRITTEN WORD that He left us as an inheritance of FAITH, aiming at our improvement!

Therefore, we insist on remembering here the origin of all this knowledge, whenever we have an opportunity, without losing focus, because it is part of this study's essence and the POWER that we want to access and absorb in this interesting EXPERIENCE.

It gathers all knowledge for those who have it to conquer their dreams, goals, and plans to create, produce, build, develop, and undertake to prosper and make everything around them prosper. With it, we can change strategies, tactics, and directions without losing focus, efficiency, and direction of the path we are following. Achieving and surpassing our goals, so that in the end we find our victory and have the conditions to maintain success, in addition to making it pass from generation to generation, prospering our children's children.

This is an important "key" that protects and characterizes every source, making it prosper and spreading to its descendants through the ages.

All of this is the result of the WISDOM acquired with the excellence of the EXPERIENCE lived!

Also, it gives us talents, according to the vocation of each one of us, so that we can employ them with dedication and discipline:

In studies, in sports, in the functions we exercise, in the careers we follow, in the professions we develop, in the various types of work, in business, in ideas, in inventions, in creation and production, in volunteering, in philanthropy or in social action that we employ; in the various projects we create or participate in, in short, in everything we do, and especially in all activities that have the purpose of generating common prosperity both for us and for the society in which we are inserted and sharing this GIVEN GIFT that descends from GREATER FAITH!

EXPERIENCE can consolidate discernment within us and give us the extraordinary vision that makes us see far beyond what is apparent and even the ability to unravel what is hidden from our perception, within each information, with extreme precision and enormous efficiency.

It is dependent on each of our levels of discipline and dedication.

Because that is the principal rule of EXPERIENCE.

Now, please, calmly, concentrate, and follow the words that represent a peaceful and suggestive thought of peace that will lead us to a dimension of harmony:

There is a certain virtue within each EXPERIENCE, which we need to find, firmly embrace, and apply it, never to lose it again. And the name of that virtue is PATIENCE!

It is also born with us and remains faithfully cheering for us, contemplating our journey with all serenity and deep peace, just waiting for us to discover it. So that, from then on, it can acti- vate its great and generous power, overflowing with compassion and mercy, in our lives.

Which will certainly result in something tre- mendous, in a truly fascinating event, built together with EXPERIENCE and FAITH that in unity will generate within each one of us, the HOPE that WINS fear!

It is full of WISDOM, PATIENCE, JUSTICE, and INTELLIGENCE, and all the VIRTUES of a fantastic LIFE! We must always pay close attention to the circumstances until we find the virtues that teach us, perfect us, and create in us the fantastic POWER of WISDOM, gen- erating the EXPERIENCE that expands our

INTELLIGENCE and makes us overcome adversities, strengthening our PERSONALITY with extraordinary COURAGE!

It is fascinating and important to emphasize that all the EXPERIENCES that we live give us the possibility to reinvent ourselves, to change the course, without losing the way; we changed the course understanding that there is a better path during our journey that will make us reach our peak more safely.

Often, this change in direction, which we are dealing with here, will take us longer to reach our goals; other times, quite the opposite. Such a change, of course, will enable us to arrive faster and achieve our goals in a much shorter time.

However, at all times, it will bring us a new EXPERIENCE and a new beginning because you must never believe that it is over.

After all, every end brings with it a new beginning!

In a very subtle, almost imperceptible way, the EXPERIENCES that we acquire, more and more, gradually shape and strengthen our spirit and our soul, producing and injecting more energy into our mind and vitality to our body.

And, thus, invigorating our whole being!

After all, we were all "planted" on this extraordinary Earth, where we were born, giving continuity to the human species, where we grow and develop. We bear our fruits right here on this beautiful Blue Planet to live the incredible experience, which translates into this great gift that is the wonderful life!

Never give up on life!

Never allow them to steal your smile and your happiness!

Never give in to discouragement!

Because your journey doesn't end here!

Use wisely all the knowledge you have acquired with the various EXPERIENCES you have lived in.

Pay attention to everything!

Remember all the good that you've lived!

Keep alive in your memories only what brings you joy and generates hope!

Try to enjoy 100% (one hundred per-cent) of everything you live. Do the same in everything while you still live!

Build your tomorrow, living well and healthier today!

Celebrate every day for being alive in this won-derful thing called life!

Live intensely day-to-day and always seek the best for your life.

Remember that we were born, we grow up, we develop, and we live this fantastic experience of life where we are perfected in this incredible Earth!

In this world in which our years pass quickly, and soon we fly to the stars in the vastness of the sky, back home, to the Eternal Kingdom, prepared for us by GOD, from the beginning!

So, make sure that you have already won.

No matter what your predicament is, you are no longer hostage to death because you've received the chance to enter the extraordinary experience of winning the Grace of GOD, through the hands of the ETERNAL JESUS, THE CHRIST!

AND HE IS the One who lived all human experiences and limitations, making the immense ultimate sacrifice for LOVE to all of us, dying on the cross for our sins, and consequently overcoming death and all other things. HE has RISEN!

HE changed our history, bringing us from the condemnation of death, enabling us salvation for eternal life with Him, through the magnificent opportunity that gives all who believe to achieve redemption and reconciliation with our Creator, ETERNAL GOD!

Give importance to the details, because each one of them has the surprising gift of providing you with unexpected joy and even healing inner peace!

Try to take a moment every day to chat with GOD.

Create the smart habit and the strong experience of looking inside yourself, in order to improve your behavior, so that you can find the virtues and answers that will help to shape your improvement.

Look at the sky more, because you may be surprised by the inspiration and the motivating force that descends from there to fill your life!

Get in the habit of planting good seeds of peace wherever you walk. Include these experiences!

Plant a tree!

Write a book!

Fall in love!

Truly love!

Build a beautiful Family!

Live a beautiful love story!

Appreciate and value good people!

Always seek what is best, without losing simplicity and without committing the sin of vanity!

Do your best to build your best experience in this life.

And how do you build a good experience?

Especially not forgetting the rich teaching of paying attention to the important details, in each of your "footprints" for life.

Use it to breakthrough!

Use it to overcome!

Use it to win!

Use your EXPERIENCE to build courage, and also use it to destroy.

Destroy what?

Destroy fear!

Did you know that many people do not win because they are unconsciously afraid to win?

Others do not win because they believe in the word of discouragement, which unfortunately every day, in all media and all forms of mass communication, is broadcast and propagated on all continents to undermine our self-esteem.

It is unfortunate to see that infinitely more words of discouragement and bad news are actually disseminated than words of encouragement and good news.

React and fight it all!

Be a carrier, a propagator, and the spokesperson for inspiring words, those that generate good spirits, and always bring motivating good news with you!

Try to reflect on any news that comes to you, exercise philosophy's experience, and question everything in search of "seeing" the truth that may be hidden within each information.

Examine, using a "magnifying glass," from the headline to each news item's end. You have that right, so always use it respecting contrary opinions with all the warmth, serenity, and wisdom!

Try to think and even manage to look at the world as you would like it to be!

Remember your beautiful innocent smile when you were a child!

And a child's smile says much more than we can even imagine!

The EXPERIENCE is revitalizing!

It does not let you be held hostage by adversity or tribulation that cause fear, anguish and disappointment. Because EXPERIENCE produces HOPE!

That is the topic that we will address in the next chapter.

Turn the page, "literally," turn the page of discouragement and live an amazing EXPERIENCE that is LIFE, because it will bring you a"valuable gift " that is HOPE!

Observe nature, how beautiful it is!

I can't get enough of looking at it, and feeling all its incredible magic it uses to exclaim all that!

And what is most fantastic, and incredibly extraordinary, in this strong, impacting and impressive EXPERIENCE of life here in this dimension, is the fact that GOD created our entire World and the infinite Universe, in just six days. So that on the seventh day he could stop and contemplate his magnificent and incomparable work, the genesis of everything!

There is a purpose for everything under the infinite sky!

We are all born with a mysterious purpose that will reveal itself throughout life's experiences!

And believe me, there is a purpose for your life!

Keep your best instincts sharp, enhance your senses and expand your vision!

Seeing how great our journey has been so far in a place called HOPE is what we will unveil at this moment of the journey in search of the knowledge that leads us to improvement through WISDOM's skillful hands.

However, we well know that FAITH, HOPE, AND LOVE go together. They are powerful to transform all situations, bringing into existence the realization of the impossible, in our lives, through the SUPERNATURAL. POWER OF THE ALIVE AND ETERNAL GOD!

By which they manifest:

Miracles!

Spectacles!

Wonders!

Since before the beginning of Genesis that we know of.

Because before all things exist, there is the Word, the Great I AM!

And, with all these POWERFUL FORCES in our lives, we will certainly have a great and unforgettable journey, marked supernaturally by them, where every moment will pave our way towards VICTORY!

That VICTORY that was prophesied to us in the Old Testament and revealed in the New Testament of the Bible with the glorious presence of JESUS CHRIST, its greatest expression being materialized by His RESURRECTION and ASCENSION TO HEAVEN where he came from!

And from where he will return to seek us to meet Him in heaven, fulfilling our rapture, as he promised us. IT IS HE WHO keeps this "flame" of HOPE burning inside us, remembering that He overcame death for us, the death that was our greatest fear!

Chapter 14

FAITH AND PATIENCE STRENGTHENS THE EFFICIENCY OF HOPE

HOPE IS A FANTASTIC THING!
IT'S A SUPERNATURAL THING!

It balances our whole being and emotional system. Because all our emotions are balanced and harmonized by HOPE, it brings us PEACE!

HOPE is generated in us by the POWER OF FAITH, lived through our EXPERIENCES!

And to have this gift, we need a lot of FAITH and PATIENCE! So far we've seen that by defeating anxiety, we gain SELF DOMAIN.

And with SELF DOMAIN, WE EXERCISE THE STRENGTH OF SELF-ESTEEM.

WITH THE STRENGTH OF SELF-ESTEEM, WE BREAK THROUGH THE STORM and whatever else tries to afflict us!

BREAKING THE STORM, we see the LIGHT of solution, as we have studied and reflected here in this book in its specific chapter.

And seeing the LIGHT OF THE SUN, we give a LEAP OF FAITH that we need to apply the solution, fight, overcome adversity, and all other circumstances with COURAGE!

We believe that it is from there that we learn to live courageously to have every chance of truly winning.

And living with COURAGE, we take unexpected actions many times, but in a very well calculated way for ourselves, we make perfect SACRIFICES for a greater good.

So, when we practice such things, we acquire WISDOM, valuable WISDOM!

And so, we receive all the virtues and gifts it gives us, including the essential and almost infinite power of creativity!

And so, endowed with WISDOM, we challenge an old enemy described in chapter 10 of this book, the enemy that was known by the name of the *problem*, the one we killed in chapter 10, remember?

And in the place of that deceased enemy, a great ally was born that motivates us strongly and impels us to face and overcome the difficulties and obstacles that stand in the way of our journey.

Over time, this ally has also revealed itself as a faithful friend called CHALLENGE, and all its synonyms together form the new meaning we have learned to use to label any adversity.

Understanding that CHALLENGE made us realize that we no longer have the old enemy "*problem*," the one that insisted on coming against us to try to intimidate us, because he left exactly as we saw in this study that we did in the referred chapter.

We didn't stop there. We proceeded to the "target" with much more strength and enthusiasm, realizing that after having received all this greater motivation that FAITH and COURAGE give us, with which we faced, crossed and won the tribulation with our head high, equipped with this strong armor and that powerful armament that we conquered along this extraordinary path!

So, from this point on we are AWAKENED by the STRENGTH OF PERSEVERANCE that BUILDS on us, EXPERIENCE with FAITH AND PATIENCE!

After all, EXPERIENCE, as we well know, is the collection of everything we live or experience! And in an incredible, fantastic and extraordinary way, EXPERIENCE produces HOPE!

Therefore, we now have the chance to experience this great POWER that makes us much stronger and even INVULNERABLE!

Able to cancel all the weak points of our emotions, generating a resistance so strong that it can even make us overcome everything that previously afflicted us, if we act with FAITH, PATIENCE, COURAGE, FIRMNESS AND INTEGRITY!

Just contemplating this immense "SEA" full of VIRTUES, fills my HEART with JOY and HOPE, my SOUL breathes relieved and the HOLY SPIRIT OF GOD, who dwells in me, rejoices, celebrates and announces that a sweet VICTORY is in the air!

Keep FAITH and take possession of HOPE, because VICTORY is in the air!

HOPE IS THE ANTIDOTE that Cures us from the poison of fear and makes us OVERCOME!

IT RESTORES US!

IT makes us relive!

IT RESURRECTS our DREAMS!

IT RETURNS US PEACE!

Because HOPE is born out of the POWER OF FAITH!

We can never forget that HOPE perfects us and brings us PATIENCE, SERENITY and calms us, developing our SOUL the ASSURANCE that we are on the right path, and what we really seek and need, we will achieve, conquer or receive.

And, it is precisely at that time that HOPE gives us the POWER to BELIEVE that better days are SURE to come!

That at dawn we will have a new opportunity and that we will never perish because the STRENGTH and its LIGHT cover us!

Through the doors of MERCY and the COMPASSION of GOD Himself, who enveloped us with his infinite GRACE and eternal LOVE, in a greater and incomparable attitude, revealed through His Only Begotten Son, namely: our Master; Savior, Friend; King of Kings; and Lord of Lords; JESUS CHRIST!

So, for all that we have witnessed so far, we can calmly declare that with the POWER of FAITH, HOPE OVERCOMES fear!

Chapter 15

*WITH THE
POWER OF FAITH*

We will go a little deeper to improve our knowledge about FAITH. We will review the foundation and great strength of this important theme. It has surprised humanity throughout the ages, from its extraordinary POWER to move all the impossible things for us, just as easily as we move everything possible for us, bringing into existence what is invisible as if it were visible.

It brings into existence what does not exist as if it already existed!

How magnificent is Your POWER! Just as it is written in the New Testament Gospels, of our Christian Bible, in the letter of the Apostle Paul to the Hebrews, in Chapter 11.

The Lord JESUS taught him and inspired him to share this fantastic teaching with us, which powerfully translates FAITH's great meaning for the edification of our lives.'

And as we begin this reading, we are quickly impacted by the power of the word of GOD, from verse 1, of chapter 11, of this strong letter from the Apostle Paul to the Hebrews, saying:

"Now faith is confidence in what we hope for and assurance about what we do not see."

It is exceptional and at the same time remarkable everything that our ancestors, the unforgettable Heroes of FAITH, lived!

When we imagine all this, we marvel at the great achievements of the power of FAITH.

This experience is so strong that it leaves us with another exceptional legacy, which is FIDELITY.

We understand that for our FAITH to be alive and generate the most surprising results in our lives, we must first make an intelligent choice, the important decision-making process called ATTITUDE. THE ATTITUDE to BELIEVE, WITHOUT DOUBT, with all the FIRMNESS and INTEGRITY of THOUGHT. Only then will our behavior reflect our FAITH under the circumstances.

Never forget that FAITH is, first and foremost, a matter of ATTITUDE! FAITH is so powerful that in addition to blessing those who have it, it is also capable of performing miracles in the lives of those who are in the company of those who have it, even though they do not yet have it.

Let us look at the example of the miracle that General Naaman received from GOD by the FAITH of his servants, who convinced him to obey the guidance of the Prophet Elisha, as it is written in the Old Testament of the Bible, in 2 Kings 5: 9 - 14. It is worth mentioning here the verse 14 of 2 Kings, chapter 5, to enrich our study on the POWER OF FAITH:

"So he went down and dipped himself in the Jordan seven times, as the man of God had told him, and his flesh was restored and became clean like that of a young boy."

How magnificent was this miracle that GOD, through His wonderful Grace, through the Prophet Elisha, gave to Naaman, when he completely healed him from the wounds caused by the leprosy that had taken over his body!

Repeating the fact that Naaman was healed by GOD, by the FAITH of his servants, who believed and convinced him to obey what the Prophet Elisha prescribed to him, so that he could be fully healed. It is a strong and inspiring testimony of the POWER OF FAITH in GOD put into action!

Crowning our understanding, during this reflection experience, to generate the awakening of FAITH for some and the revival of FAITH for others, it is important to highlight that all this translates into the great meaning of the name "JESUS," which is GOD SAVES!

How tremendous and extraordinary it is to believe this truth!

Understanding that which we inherited from GOD when we studied His Words and took possession of the great meanings contained in each one, as they are written in the Holy Scriptures.

As we have just examined the POWER of FAITH experienced by our ancestors, as described in this letter of the Apostle Paul to the Hebrews, which is so perfect that we made a point of including his chapter 11 here, to enlighten us with the same WISDOM that JESUS inspired him with, guiding him to write it and thus also eternalize the propagation of this Gospel from generation to generation so that they could be perfected with FAITH and thus we will achieve SALVATION because HE LOVES us!

And, even today, because of His eternal LOVE, many miracles continue to happen by the POWER of FAITH.

My family and I were the targets of the Grace of GOD. We are witnesses of this divine extraordinary phenomenon that made us realize the impossible.

But this, too, is one of many other good testimonies that we will share in another story. Because FAITH brings with it this Grace that is the favor we receive from GOD even though we do not deserve it.

Because the Grace of GOD is an undeserved favor!

As a testimony, my family and I will share one of FAITH and Miracle's experiences for the Grace of GOD, which we live and also live with a young woman and her family, at an extraordinary stage of our lives.

All this miracle brings to mind a similar experience, which I had with my family in Church.

Where a family of a very dear friend of ours, like many others who gathered with us at that time, a young teenager was suffering from a mysterious illness that caused the appearance of several wounds on her body.

Now, she was already being treated by the best doctors that money could afford because her parents spared no resources and invested all their efforts in seeking their daughter's cure.

However, mysteriously, the wounds on her body did not heal, and quite the contrary, they continued to multiply, spreading through her body, causing her pain, immense embarrassment, and strong discomfort, damaging her day-to-day and even weakening her defense system, weakening your health.

When I saw this young woman suffering so much, my "heart cried, and it hurt" with compassion because, in a very personal and supernatural way, I could feel at that moment the pain and how badly she was suffering.

I remember, I was standing beside Sônia, my wife, and our little girl Vitória, who was still a little child. I really felt the pain of that young girl, who could not dress as she would like to dress because of the open wounds, and when covering her wounds, she felt pain and everything else that a terrible disease like this can cause. So, I stopped everything, concentrated, raised my thoughts to JESUS and talked to HIM, and with GOD Himself, through HIM, I prayed, crying, asking for her cure.

And an impressive fact is that in that period of time, I was on a personal quest, and a spiritual purpose with JESUS so that GOD would give me vulnerability to the afflictions of this world.

Holiness; a portion of holiness that would make me see what really matters to our lives, and so that I would have the gift and the ability to use HIS FAITH, HOPE, and LOVE service, as JESUS taught me, together with my family to save lives.

At that moment, I felt a wonderful presence of him giving me a special inspiration and the anointing of GOD, to intercede and to continue interceding in prayer, so that HE would heal that young woman.

Then, I talked with the Pastor of the Church, at that time, to ask for his opinion regarding this inspiration of FAITH that I had experienced, of the action to pray, and to raise a cry to GOD, for the healing of that young girl, of our community. I narrated all of this to him in detail then asked him:

Pastor, do you agree to continue with us on a face-to-face purpose for healing this young woman, if she and her parents agree?

And he immediately took pity on the situation and confidently said to me: if GOD inspired you, then this is your purpose.

I can only join you in prayer, but it is you that He has CALLED, so it is up to you to "battle" for her cure. From then on, The Pastor, my wife Sonia and I spoke to the young girl and her parents, they were very dear to us. We told them what GOD had inspired us to use our FAITH to pray for her healing.

And suddenly, it came to my mind to purposefully pray for 21 days and intercede with JESUS, with that young woman and her family. I still remember that I declared with all certainty that before we completed the 21 days, she would be completely healed of that terrible and mysterious illness, without any scars, and that all the open wounds that this young woman had on her body, from her head to the soles of her feet, would disappear without a trace.

Both she and her excellent parents, agreed and believed.

They already knew me, they knew my family, we congregated in the same Christian Community, where we were neighbors, and that is what we did.

We arranged to meet in person at their home, once a week, on Wednesdays. So, Sonia and I got ready for this "spiritual warfare," through fasting and prayer, interceding and crying out in the name of JESUS CHRIST, so that GOD could perform this great miracle, pouring out His healing in that young woman's life.

On the very first day, while we cried out for her cure, I knelt and put my hands on her feet, imagining all the pain she felt because she couldn't even step firmly on the ground. She had open wounds on the soles of her feet. At that moment, tears came down my cheeks. But, at the same time, I felt an intense heat, and then a profound peace, a supernatural refreshment that certainly was brought by the glorious presence of JESUS CHRIST.

We continued to persevere in prayer for this purpose of FAITH. Well, before we reached the halfway point of those 21 days, the healing of the wounds was already visible.

The wounds were closing, they were drying, killing all that inflammation, making all pain there before to heal, and GOD was healing her.

Because the LOVE of GOD revealed in His Son JESUS CHRIST, the strongest way that GOD chose to reveal himself to us, anointed us, and HE HEALED that girl totally, before the end of the 21 days all the wounds had healed, and the marks disappeared, and she was healed.

FAITH in GOD, through JESUS CHRIST, is a powerful "weapon," capable of accomplishing great deeds: Miracles, Spectacles, and Wonders, and everything impossible could become possible.

Because when your purpose is good, you do your part and take an attitude of FAITH, nobody can stop you, as we have also seen here in this book, which works to bring to mind a glimpse of the POWER and GLORY of GOD, for the salvation of our lives by His ETERNAL WORD, as he left us written in the Holy Scriptures that mark and cross-time through the history of us all.

When your purpose is good, nobody can stop you!

You can be sure that you will have the victory in the end, no matter if you have to go through the Valley and the Desert. We know that they are dark territories because these Valleys are dark places, they are hot, and they are also cold and full of venomous and poisonous creatures, hidden dangers, and everything else that is bad in the Valley.

So much so that this valley we are dealing with here is also the one described by King David, as the Valley of the Shadow of Death, within Psalms 23, inspired by GOD, in the Old Testament, where it reveals this strong message of FAITH, with an emphasis on verse 4, saying:

"Even though I walk through the darkest valley, I will fear no evil, for you are with me; your rod and your staff, they comfort me."

This is the parallel we are making here concerning the Valley and the Desert, with our adversities and the dangers we face, in the midst of great difficulties, "test in the fire," fights and battles, representing all challenges and tribulations we face in our time.

Then you realize that Deserts are also similar to Valleys.

Deserts are scorching during the day and extremely cold at night. Also full of all kinds of deadly dangers.

But with FAITH in JESUS CHRIST, we will cross Deserts and Valleys, because we will not be alone; HE will be with us, because we decided to honor Him in Love, in Truth, and in Spirit, Loving GOD with all our strength!

And the HOLY and ETERNAL GOD will lead us in complete safety, as it is written in the Old Testament, in Psalms 91.

We are certain and guarantee that GOD will always be with us and will protect us, as it is also written in Psalms 91:15, where HE tells us:

"He will call on me, and I will answer him; I will be with him in trouble, I will deliver him and honor him."

FAITH is a great power that connects with the thought and will of GOD that brings things into existence. All we need is to truly believe for the fulfillment of the purposes of integrity and holiness.

Chapter 16

WITH THE POWER OF FAITH, HOPE OVERCOMES FEAR!

Once upon a time, a beautiful girl named Ela was walking in a beautiful garden, and it was a sunny spring morning with a perfect "symphony" of birds humming beautiful songs. Simultaneously, a fine, white, almost totally transparent mist brought the sweet scent of the abundant flowers, leaves, and fruits!

She was very sad and even crying as she remembered, missing an extraordinary someone who was part of her life ever since birth. This great friend was HOPE!

She cried out to GOD to bring her friend back into her life, for she had lost her way from her faithful best friend HOPE that had disappeared.

Suddenly, she felt a gentle breeze of wind blowing in a very different way, and peculiar over her head, causing a feeling of deep peace!

She heard a soft and very familiar voice that made her heart race and even vibrated with emotion!

That soft voice brought by the breeze of the wind was actually her best friend's voice;

It was the voice of HOPE, which she had lost and was "missing" for a long, long time in her life!

That serene, calm and soft voice of her Friend came from the right side of that beautiful and flowered garden, calling for her, restoring her joy, and stopping her tears, to an immediately beautiful smile, instead!

In that "magic" hour, when she turned to the right side of this beautiful garden, looked and saw her great friend coming towards her;

She was ecstatic!

HOPE came smoothly, almost supernaturally, and stopped right in front of her;

This extraordinary moment impacted her with a feeling of incomparable happiness and, at the same time, so emotional and difficult for her to utter a word!

She took a deep breath and hugged her faithful friend HOPE strongly, saying: Today is the happiest day of my life because you are back here with me!

How wonderful!

My best friend who was "missing" has now resurfaced to save me and prevent me from leaving this beautiful garden and dying in the "Valley of the shadow of death," which fell on all the earth right after we lost you, HOPE!

"Do not be afraid," Hope said, "because I am here with you!"

HOPE, thank you so much for coming back to me!

For not forgetting me!

Hope replied, "Ela, I would never forget you."

Thank goodness, HOPE!

I will never lose you again!

When you were gone, I was very discouraged and even crying, with immense sadness, regretting that I'd lost you and caused you to "disappear" from my life.

Honestly, I had the absurd idea that I was dead.

But thanks to GOD, you, my great friend, are here as alive, strong, radiant, and beautiful as before I lost you!

HOPE looked right into Ela's eyes, with enormous compassion and tenderness; with that "Divine and confident look", that only HOPE has, and asked:

Ela, my friend, did you forget who I am?

I come from GOD, who IS Eternal! Therefore, I am also eternal!

Because whoever is from GOD, is also eternal and never dies!

Very moved by the revelation that HOPE had just made to her, Ela asked: HOPE, now that you're back, I won't feel any more fear?

HOPE responded saying: Because you cried out to GOD and HE brought me back into your life.

Happy and with enormous gratitude to GOD and also to her Friend, Ela celebrating with an innocent smile, hand in hand with HOPE, said:

HOPE, then, that means, that just as I had no fear at all, after I met you, and lived happily before I lost you. Now that I have found you, will I not be afraid again?

And HOPE replied again, to Her, saying:

Yes, Ela, you are right, my sweet friend.

Because when I arrive and stay in your life, all your fears are defeated!

At this moment, Ela felt a peace fill her whole being. Speechless, for an instant, due to the strong impact of great joy that that feeling of peace had brought to her "heart." Ela, do you now understand how it works, my friend?

And she answered exclaiming:

Glory to the ETERNAL GOD, who created HOPE for me, and for bringing you back into my life!

Today, having learned this powerful truth, which you have just revealed to me, I can declare that my Faith built up so strong that I can feel its effect within my Soul and my Spirit.

And now, I feel my self-esteem being reborn!

Today, without a doubt, is the happiest day of my life!

I will never forget this day, my friend!

I know that you were sent by GOD, my eternal Friend HOPE, who wins and makes me overcome all my fears!

This story inspires us and reminds us that GOD brings to our dimension of existence the understanding of FAITH, HOPE, and His Agape

LOVE Agape, with which HE and His Only Begotten Son, JESUS, created us in His image and resemblance from the beginning.

JESUS gives us a vision, a glimpse of what that immense LOVE is like, in the revelation of His WORD, which is in the Old Testament of our Christian Bible, in the first letter of the Apostle Paul to the Corinthians, within his chapter 13: 4 - 8a, where it is written:

"Love is patient, love is kind. It does not envy, it does not boast, it is not proud. It does not dishonor others, it is not self-seeking, it is not easily angered, it keeps no record of wrongs. Love does not delight in evil but rejoices with the truth. It always protects, always trusts, always hopes, always perseveres. Love never fails."

And His love moves us!

Because if we call GOD, in the name of His Son, JESUS CHRIST, with the Power of FAITH, the

HOPE that He has planted within each of us overcomes all of our fears!

It's at this happy moment, when we arrive in this dimension of the supernatural of GOD, to further consolidate our knowledge, establishing our steps on the eternal rock of JESUS CHRIST, sealed with His HOLY SPIRIT, meditate on the message that disciplines us with POWER FROM THE FATHER, simplifies our search for understanding the true meaning of life. Revealing its extraordinary meaning, which is also written in the Old Testament of our Christian Bible, in the first letter of the Apostle Paul to the Corinthians, within its chapter 13, in verse 13, exclaiming:

"And now these three remain: faith, hope and love. But the greatest of these is love."

After all, it is worth emphasizing and remembering here a straightforward formula, and at the same time very effective, distributed throughout the chapter titles of this book. We have taken the strong and faithful proposal of repeating them on the path we have taken. In the light of wisdom and the fruit of experience, to discern everything and practice these teachings in our lives.

Declaring with all firmness and integrity, that dwells within each one of us, the Holy Spirit of GOD! And it is with Him that our HOPE lives forever and prevails: * Defeating anxiety * * GAINING SELF DOMAIN * * EXERCISING THE STRENGTH OF SELF-ESTEEM * * BREAKING the "storm" * * THE ILLUMINATING SUN * * Taking a leap of faith * * LIVING WITH COURAGE * * MAKING SACRIFICES * * ACQUIRING WISDOM * * CHALLENGING and eliminating the problem * * Facing tribulations with faith and courage * * WITH THE STRENGTH OF PERSEVERANCE * * WITH THE FRUIT OF EXPERIENCE * * WITH FAITH AND PATIENCE STRENGTHENING THE EFFICIENCY OF HOPE * * BY THE POWER OF FAITH *

* BECAUSE WITH THE POWER OF FAITH, HOPE OVERCOMES FEAR! *